Vet on the Loose

Gillian Hick was born in Dublin and has practised as a vet both in Dublin and in Wicklow for the past seven years. She also works for the Irish Blue Cross. She lives in Co. Wicklow, where she has her own practice, with her husband, three children, and a large assortment of four-legged companions. *Vet on the Loose* is her first book.

VET ON THE
LOOSE

Gillian Hick

THE O'BRIEN PRESS
DUBLIN

First published 2005 by The O'Brien Press Ltd,
20 Victoria Road, Dublin 6, Ireland.
Tel: +353 1 4923333; Fax: +353 1 4922777
E-mail: books@obrien.ie
Website: www.obrien.ie

ISBN: 0-86278-925-7

British Library Cataloguing-in-Publication Data
A catalogue reference for this book is available from the British Library.

While this book is drawn from actual experience over several years of practice,
situations, locations and names have been changed.
Any resemblance to any person is entirely accidental.

1 2 3 4 5 6 7 8 9 10
05 06 07 08 09 10

Editing, typesetting, layout and design: The O'Brien Press Ltd
Illustrations: cover and page 1: Martyn Turner; page 2: Aidan Cooney
Printing: Nørhaven Paperback A/S

Acknowledgements

Thanks must go, first of all, to the animals who unwittingly surrendered themselves to the ministrations of a novice vet. Without them this story could never have been told. To Slug, my faithful companion on the journey through veterinary medicine. Many thanks to the owners of Jill, the collie; they allowed her story to be told as it actually happened – all the other animals, though drawn from experience, are fictitious, and are amalgams formed from my experience.

To Joe and Claire Kelly, my parents, for proof-reading – and much, much more. Thanks to the many veterinary colleagues and readers who contributed to the overall final outcome; especially to Vanessa. Thanks to the staff of O'Brien Press for working deadlines around three pre-school children and a veterinary practice.

A special thanks must go to Tom Kelly, veterinary colleague, editor and friend, for many, many phone-calls, e-mails and moral support. Any inaccuracies, bad grammar or worse still remaining in the text are there only because I was too stubborn to change them. (At least, I left out the snow scenes!)

Finally, to Donal, my husband, and Molly, Fiona and Jack – thanks for putting up with me writing when I could have been – and probably should have been – doing a hundred and one other things.

CONTENTS

PROLOGUE

The very first horse castration I ever performed as a veterinary surgeon was in the depths of Dublin's inner city. But as I drove around the urban jungle on the appointed morning, I was convinced that I must have been given the wrong address. When I finally found 53, Primrose Villas it was an ordinary, terraced house located on a narrow street, and a most unlikely looking setting in which to find a horse.

Where could the horse be? I wondered, looking warily around the tiny front garden that wouldn't even have been big enough to contain a car, had there been one. All seemed to be deserted and there was no reply when I hammered on the front door, after a futile search for a doorbell.

I was about to leave when a child's voice yelled out through the open window above me: 'Are you the vet?'

'That's right!' I called back up. 'Are your parents home?'

'What's it to you? I haven't done nuttin',' he replied, before disappearing behind the shabby net curtain.

I waited for him to reappear at the front door but had to hammer again before I heard a shuffling inside and the door opened a crack.

'Are ye here for de horse or wha'?'

'Yes, that's right,' I replied as pleasantly as I could. 'Where do you keep him?'

'Come 'ere,' he answered, gesturing over his shoulder for me to follow him through the kitchen and on out through the back door to a patch of muck no bigger than the front garden.

In these unpromising surroundings it was incongruous to see the tiny stallion, in all his piebald glory, happily relaxing in the sun, surrounded by old bikes, torn rubbish sacks and the battered remains of a long-abandoned television set.

'Right, so,' I managed, trying to hide my amazement. 'Are your parents around so we can get started?'

'It's *my* bleedin' horse. Wha' d'ye wan' me aul' ones for? It's nuttin' to do with dem.'

'Well, we'll need them to give us a hand.'

'Are ye jokin'? Me Ma's terrified of 'im and she's out anyways.'

'What about your Dad? Where's he?'

'As if I'd bleedin' know!' came the scornful reply. 'Haven't seen that geezer in years.' The boy stared at me balefully as though challenging me to reply.

I was beginning to feel a vague sense of disbelief. I had always imagined that my first horse castration would be performed in a fancy yard, full of competent handlers, the magnificent stallion skilfully restrained as I carried out the routine surgery in serene silence, broken only by the occasional ripple of approving murmurs from the impressed onlookers. But it looked like it was to be just myself, young Eddie, and Anto the piebald.

I hesitated for a moment and then decided we might as well get on with it.

'Right, so. Could you get me a big basin full of hot water, please, and we'll need a rope to hold him with.'

'Okay, Doctor,' replied young Eddie, clearly pleased that the show was under way.

While he was gone, I carefully filled my syringes with anaesthetic, anti-tetanus, antibiotic and the local anaesthetic to inject into the testicles.

Eddie was chuffed with himself as he staggered back under the weight of the washing-up basin, the water sloshing all over the place so that by the time he got to me, it was half-empty. I carefully fished a few baked beans and a piece of soggy toast out of the water that was supposedly going to sterilise my equipment. I added a dash of iodine and hoped that might do the trick.

'What about a head-collar, Eddie?' I asked. 'You'll need something to hold him with.'

His face briefly deepened into a frown and then, without a further thought, he carelessly pulled a Stanley knife out of his back pocket and with one practised slash, cut the rope that had served as a washing line to make a halter.

'Won't your mother kill you for doing that?' I inquired curiously, as he piled the half-dry washing in a heap on the edge of the rubbish pile that was threatening to overtake the entire garden.

He shrugged nonchalantly, with the air of one who was

well used to being in trouble. 'Sure, Jaysus, she's always moanin' about somethin'.'

'All right, Eddie, you get a good hold of him now and I'll give him his first injection.'

Thankfully, Anto was a placid type and he didn't object as I rooted through the shaggy coat until I found the jugular vein and inserted the needle. I drew back the plunger on the syringe and as a gush of fresh blood mixed through the clear liquid in the syringe, my assistant smiled for the first time. 'Ah Jaysus, yer puttin' de stuff in 'is blood. Dat's fuckin' cool, dat is, Doc.'

Well, I thought to myself, at least I have an appreciative audience.

Within minutes, the little stallion was well sedated and soon he was wobbling slightly precariously due to the effects of my generous dose of anaesthetic.

Eddie was disappointed when I tried to explain to him that this was a new type of anaesthetic and that Anto would remain standing for the duration of the surgery.

'Ye mean I won't have te sit on 'is head like I did wit me last horse?'

'No, he'll stay standing up the whole time,' I repeated, wishing I felt as confident as I sounded, watching the little stallion as he staggered drunkenly from side to side, legs threatening to buckle under him with each movement.

Quickly, I disinfected the area and injected the local anaesthetic into the testicles, starting to feel a bit dizzy myself now as I swayed in unison with his hindquarters and hoping that if he did fall, he wouldn't take me with him.

As I waited for the anaesthetic to take effect, I tried to engage in some light-hearted banter, but I didn't really know where to begin.

'You're not at school today, Eddie?'

Sullen looks. 'It's a load o' crap.'

I tried again. 'How long have you had Anto?'

'Long enough.'

'Where did you get him from?'

He glared at me suspiciously. 'From a man.'

I gave up. Obviously adults asking questions was not to be tolerated.

At last the horse was ready and as I pulled out the sharp scalpel blade, Eddie perked up again. 'Jaysus, dat looks real sharp. Can I 'ave it when yer finished?'

'Ah no, I'd need it again for another horse,' I replied quickly, despite the fact that they are strictly single-use, disposable ones.

I grasped the far testicle and incised deep into the tissue, watching with satisfaction as the glistening organ dropped out of the sack, suspended by an array of ligaments and blood vessels.

'They're bleeding massive!' came the envious sigh.

Carefully, I placed the jaws of my shiny new emasculators around the vasculature and squeezed hard until the handles met and the slow crunching sound was replaced by a quiet thud as the testicle dropped to the ground.

Eddie was ecstatic. 'Ah massive! If I put dat in me sister's bed tonight it'll scare de shite outa her!'

He was no less enthusiastic as I repeated the procedure on the other side and was now beginning to look at me with renewed respect.

Before I knew it, my first horse castration was completed. I looked contentedly at the still-staggering gelding that stood before me and even if the surroundings were not quite what I had anticipated, no audience could have been more enthusiastic than Eddie, who was now carefully examining the testicles, one in each hand.

A busy day beckoned and, sadly, I had to bring the show to an end.

'Right so,' I said to my new admirer. 'Keep an eye on him and check that there are no more than just drops of blood. Call me if you have any problem.'

'No bother so, Doc. Now, wha' do I owe ye?' he asked with the expression of a hardened dealer.

'Ninety-five euro to yourself,' I replied.

Without hesitation, he sank his blood-stained hand into his back pocket and pulled out a wad of fivers. He carefully counted out nineteen of them, pausing to lick his counting finger between each note.

'Ninety-five, so,' he said, slapping the wad into my palm and completing the deal. He hesitated for a moment and then decisively grabbed another note and stuffed it into my hand. 'And dat's for yourself, luv.'

I tried not to insult his magnanimous gesture by laughing, but the sight of the serious expression on the spiky-haired, freckle-faced youngster was too much and I had to turn away as I pocketed the notes.

This time he led me out through the side passage and watched admiringly as I packed my equipment into the boot of the car.

'Well, good luck so, Eddie, see you again,' I called out.

'D'ye know wha' it is, Doc?' he said, and paused as I awaited the verdict from my young client. 'Yer a mad feckin' bitch, that's what ye are!' he affirmed, with deep admiration glistening in the depths of his young eyes.

THE STUDENT VET

CHAPTER ONE

SEEING PRACTICE

I spent my first week in a veterinary practice as an innocent fourteen year-old when I was both honoured and thrilled to be allowed to clean out the cattery in a local small-animal practice. To handle an animal that was under the care of a vet seemed such a wonder and even an afternoon spent folding and enveloping invoices left me deliriously happy that at last I was on my way.

Watching my first cat spay from a sterile distance, I was so chuffed you could well believe I had done the surgery myself. So awed was I by the experience that I was totally dumbstruck when the vet asked me if I would like a cup of coffee and I nodded my assent even though I hated coffee at the time.

Much and all as I would have loved to go back, I didn't want to tempt fate by preparing myself for a career that might never be mine. It wasn't until my third time repeating the Leaving Certificate in search of those elusive points, that one of the teachers in the school, probably sensing my end-stage frustration as I ploughed my way through yet another Shakespearean play, put me in touch with Finbar McCarthy, her brother-in-law, a vet who had a large animal practice up in the northernmost tip of Louth.

As it was too far to travel, I was to stay with the family for a week – the week I should have been preparing for my third set of mock Leaving Cert exams.

Arriving at the red-brick house for the first time, I wondered if this was the surgery, but was soon shown the purpose-built shed that served as a clinic for the local animal population.

'It may not be as fancy as some places, but it does the job all right,' said Finbar, obviously pleased with his set-up.

He brushed away my halting thanks. 'No, it's I should be thanking you,' he assured me kindly. 'It's not everyone who wants to help out at this time of year. My own kids saw sense years ago,' he laughed, obviously well reconciled to the fact that they were not going to be following in his footsteps.

Our first call was to a ramshackle farmyard, inhabited by a weather-beaten old farmer and his herd of forty or so sucklers. It was the first time I had come into such close contact with cattle and I kept a low profile as I watched Finbar and the experienced stockman pick out the sick cow from the herd and pen her up against the shed with an old gate. One of the older cows, obviously noticing my inexperience, frisked up to me and then scampered off with an indignant bellow as Finbar shooed her away. I tried to look busy inspecting the back of the shed door that

I had dived behind for cover.

'Take her temperature there,' Finbar asked me, once the patient was confined. I thanked God that I had watched enough James Herriot films to know where to put the thermometer, but it wasn't as easy as it looked to pull up the heavy tail which seemed to be welded to the cow's rear end. I reached further down to grab the bit that was swishing violently, generously christening my spotless wet-gear with a liberal spattering of farmyard manure, and worked my way up, pausing briefly before cautiously inserting the thermometer. So far so good, I thought.

Finbar concentrated as he to listened to the cow's enormous chest with his stethoscope, and I watched expectantly, hoping he might offer to let me listen too.

A noise from behind alerted me and I watched in horror as the cow lifted her tail and squirted a stream of greeny-brown faeces in an arc behind her, expelling the thermometer along with it. There it lay, in a pile below her, just the tip of the glass sticking out. Tom let out a roar of laughter.

'Well, that's one trick ye've learnt today anyway!' he declared. 'At least, it was well protected.'

Sure enough, it was still intact as I gingerly retrieved it from where it had fallen. Thankfully, Finbar hadn't noticed my blunder as by now he was busily milking out the udder.

'Have you ever milked a cow, Gillian?' he called out from underneath.

Feeling a bit foolish, I had to admit that I hadn't.

'Well, isn't now the very time to learn? Sure, maybe Tom

could give you a demonstration while I go to the car for some antibiotics.'

Tom proceeded to explain, with surprising patience, how to close off the top of the teat between the thumb and first finger while squeezing the lower part with the remaining fingers. Although my first few attempts were awkward and clumsy, by the time Finbar returned, I was happily spraying away, delighted to have mastered this new skill so swiftly.

'Go aisy on her there, or there'll be none left for the calf,' teased Tom.

'Well, have you come to a diagnosis yet there, Doctor?' Finbar inquired of me, winking at the stockman as he did so. Observing my blank face, he continued: 'Try milking the other teat.'

I grasped it in my hand and noticed that it seemed a lot warmer than the first one. I attempted to follow the same procedure only to find that, try as I might, I couldn't get any milk out. After a few attempts, a clot burst out followed by some foul-smelling watery fluid. I jumped back as the cow kicked indignantly.

'Well, there you are now,' Tom announced triumphantly, 'your first diagnosis of mastitis!' I was glad that he had clarified the matter for me!

The next case, Tom informed me, was a heifer who had held her cleanings. I nodded sagely at this piece of information, although I had absolutely no idea what he was talking about.

As the skittish young beast ran up to us, I saw a long trail of what looked like half her intestine hanging out behind her. I was astonished that Finbar didn't appear to be overly concerned by what surely must be a hopeless case. He pulled on a large plastic glove and then another and having lubricated his gloved arm, inserted it into the heifer's rear end. I watched in disbelief as he gently manipulated the putrefied mass and slowly, it stretched to the ground before dropping altogether from the cow. The smell was overpowering and I had to move away and take a few deep breaths before I could be sure I wouldn't start to retch.

'Not a job for a Friday night,' said Finbar cheerfully.

'It's a common enough condition in cattle,' he continued as he drew off the long gloves and dipped his arms in a bucket of water to which he had added a generous splash of disinfectant. 'If the afterbirth, or the "cleanings" as it's known, takes too long to pass out, then the cow becomes sick as the toxins build up in her. They usually do well enough, though, after the cleanings are removed and the uterus is flushed out.'

* * *

By now, I was feeling thoroughly versed in the art of cattle practice, but our next call was to a stableyard, to vet a horse. As though anticipating my ignorance, Finbar explained how he would carry out the detailed examination of the horse, which a client of his was thinking of buying.

'Unfortunately, she's buying it from another client of the practice, so, if the horse fails that's two less I'll have on the books,' he added, but not looking too worried about the prospect.

The horse in question was a magnificent-looking chestnut gelding. The buyer, Linda, stood by, waiting anxiously for the verdict.

'There'd have to be lot wrong with that lad to justify failing him,' said Finbar, quietly admiring him.

With my limited experience of horses, I was a bit concerned when Finbar asked me to take the gelding out of his stable, but, like a true gentleman, the horse lowered his head for me to clip on a lead rope, having first given me a good quizzical sniff.

I watched in silent fascination as, having checked the eyes and chest, Finbar concentrated on examining each leg in turn, spending what seemed like an age poking and prodding at all the bumps and lumps that made up what I supposed was a normal limb.

After examining each leg, he would hold it up off the ground, fully flexed, for a couple of minutes and then ask me to trot the horse to the top of the yard and back again, to see if he was still sound. Even with my non-existent knowledge, I couldn't fail to notice the free-flowing movement of the animal as he trotted off each time.

Henry, as the horse was known, was then turned and backed and circled in what seemed like an endless series of tests that he obviously passed with flying colours.

'Now, just to lunge him,' said Finbar to Linda, and I was thankful when she took him from me and clipped on the long lunge-line. My only previous attempt at lunging a horse had ended up with me tied up in knots before the horse even broke into a trot.

Henry started off friskily enough, happily cantering around in large circles. Soon, however, he started to get bored with the game and frequently slowed down until Linda flicked a long whip at him.

'You go in and chase him on,' said Finbar to me. 'Keep him going.'

Off I went, enthusiastically running after the horse, waving my arms to keep him going; happy to be doing something useful. He perked up a bit and cantered on with a renewed burst of enthusiasm – but only for a few seconds. Soon I had to chase him again. I found that by standing in the one spot, I could whoosh him on as he came around each time, which was enough to keep him going until the next lap – but soon he got wise to that too and lapsed into a walk halfway around the circle. There was nothing for it but to follow after him, although he kept getting ahead of me and almost appeared to be enjoying what must have looked like a game of tag. Each time I fell behind, he slowed down again until I caught up with him and then he cantered on.

'Just a few more laps!' Finbar called out encouragingly. 'I need to hear his wind when he's going at a steady canter.'

Round and round I ran after him, as my breathing became deeper and my stomach began to lurch for the second time that day. Much more quickly than the horse, I began to tire. Soon I was only trotting half-heartedly after him and was relieved to hear Finbar eventually call out to Linda to pull him up.

I sank gratefully against the field gate, trying to catch my breath until I saw that now, Henry was off again, this time in the opposite direction.

'Just keep him going for a couple of minutes and we'll be finished.'

After two laps, I couldn't keep up with him and by the third it looked as though Henry was chasing me. When I could feel him snorting over my left shoulder, I gave up.

While Finbar carried on with the examination, I sank to the ground, frantically trying to catch my breath and wondering how I was meant to hear the horse's wind over the sound of my own desperate rasping.

Thankfully, it took a while before Finbar had filled in the certificate and wished Linda luck with her new venture. He chose not to notice as I lay slumped over a round bale of hay, waiting for the agonising pains that wracked my chest to die down.

By the time he was ready to go, I had just about recovered sufficiently to drag myself into the car.

I was relieved when Finbar told me it was time to go back to the house for tea. In the warm kitchen we did justice to the mouth-watering food prepared by Finbar's wife Andrea, who laughed as she told me that I had done well to survive the first day. Throughout the meal, their four children, ranging in ages from ten to twenty-two, passed in and out, obviously well used to yet another aspiring vet joining them at the table.

I didn't know then, that this was to be the first of many meals I would share with the family. The experience reinforced my growing conviction that I had finally found my place in life.

The week passed in a flash and all too soon I was back at school, toiling through my third set of mock Leaving Cert exams. I did reasonably well at these, but my mind was still filled with lambing ewes and lame horses. The next time I went back to Finbar's, it was as a *bona fide* veterinary student, having finally become familiar enough with French grammar, mathematical theories and Shakespearean plays to obtain the required number of points for veterinary medicine.

That summer, I left school behind me forever and immersed myself in real life – scouring calves and itchy dogs. I even calved my first cow! And all before even going to college.

CHAPTER TWO

COLLEGE DAYS

After my third time sitting the Leaving Certificate exams I was finally offered the elusive DN005 – VET MED, and it seemed that heaven had come to earth. That summer was spent in a blur of ecstasy. Nothing could dent my overwhelming enthusiasm, although at times it all seemed too unreal to be true. I took to driving the long way home from routine trips just to pass by a veterinary surgery and peer in the window, or to see a brass plate hanging on the wall.

The university prospectus arrived in due course, filled with terms like 'clinical anatomy' and 'veterinary pathology', which, although I had little idea what they meant, filled me with unprecedented excitement.

At last, on a frosty October morning, the day dawned for my life as a student of veterinary medicine to begin. I had often passed the college in Ballsbridge on the way into town but had not realised that the entrance on view was not the main one but a side door to a lab which remained permanently locked. Rattling the door and seeing no sign of life, I wondered could I possibly have got the day wrong until two other new students joined me and we fell into conversation.

'Are you really interested in animals?' began one.

'Oh, God no,' replied the other. 'I wanted to do medicine but thought for a laugh that I would put down veterinary first. I never thought I'd get the points.'

'Well, that's a relief,' replied the other. 'I wanted to do science but I filled in the wrong code in the CAO form.'

I kept my mouth shut, silently stunned by this sacrilege.

By the time we had located the correct entrance and made our way up the stairs to the lecture hall, we were late and the general introduction was in full swing.

Despite this inauspicious start, we all got into the run of things fairly quickly as freshers' week broke the ice and our lectures got underway. Before we knew it, we were well established in the routine of spending half the week on campus in Belfield doing the basic sciences along with the medical students, and then the second half of the week in the veterinary college in Ballsbridge. Here we became deeply acquainted with the body of a preserved greyhound which would accompany us on our tour of anatomy for the remainder of the year. It surprised us how fond we became of Patch, as we christened him in our first practical. We listened with scarcely disguised admiration to the second years, whose job it was to fill us in on the general run of things, and familiarise us with the necessary requirements for the year ahead.

The twenty-five-week academic year – although it

seemed to slow up and almost come to a standstill around exam time – generally flew by in a whirl of academic and social fixtures.

I almost didn't become a second-year veterinary student because, during the summer of first year, I got married. I had met Donal almost four years previously, all because of Gracie, a pony which his father grazed in a field behind my parents' house. I had often admired the pretty little Connemara cross and she enjoyed nuzzling through my pocket for the slice of apple that I always brought her. I had met Donal's father by chance one day while out walking in the fields with my dogs. When he told me that he drove down twice a day to check Gracie, the mare, I offered to do it for him, delighted to get a chance to be involved.

When Gracie foaled the following summer, I met Donal. From then on, we both took a huge interest in Star, the foal, and diligently met up most days to handle him and discuss his progress despite the fact that I was supposedly studying for the Leaving Cert. By the time Star was old enough to begin his training in long reins, we had got into the habit of meeting daily and we used to spend many hours each evening walking the back roads with him. Gradually, we took to going out to buy tack for him and then to the local horse shows under the pretext of checking out the competition.

By then, Star had a little brother, Maxwell, and so our meetings became even more frequent. I don't think anyone was surprised when we finally started going out without the horses. Around the time Merlin, the third foal, appeared, we decided to get married and give the mare a break.

Back at college, I was advised to change my name to avoid confusion at a later date. I followed directions and duly notified the registrar. However, when second year started, it turned out that the authorities, in their wisdom, had deleted me from the register under my former name of Gillian Kelly but had failed to re-enter me on the register as Gillian Hick. It took a lot of persuasion, and finally a letter from the dean of the veterinary college, to convince the authorities in Belfield that I was indeed a *bona fide* veterinary student.

That year, we left Belfield behind and were established full-time in the veterinary college. The year focused mainly on animal husbandry and especially on the farm end of things. Our weekly visits out to UCD's research farm at Lyons Estate in Kildare were supposed to introduce us to the management of cattle, sheep and horses and level out the differences between those students reared in a farming background and the impostors like myself – a born and reared Dub. In anatomy, Patch was replaced by a stunted-looking Hereford cow and a small chestnut pony.

During this second year, much of the holidays were spent doing what was known as farm experience, where we went out to work on farms to learn the basic concepts of animal management from the skilled stockmen who, in a few short years, would hopefully become our clients.

The other main subject for second year was the combined physiology/biochemistry course which had the highest failure rate for that year. Three-hour written exams were followed by two sets of practicals and then, finally, just to really see if you would crack under the pressure, each student had a twenty-minute oral exam with three of the professors who would decide your fate.

To this day, the way I felt the morning of that exam is always the barometer by which I assess how much pressure I am under. Of the three interviewers, one was a lecturer with whom I got on reasonably well, the second was the head of the department and the third was an external examiner – a departmental head from an English college, brought in to standardise the results.

The biochemistry questions went fine as I managed to conjure up the required metabolic pathways, although I wouldn't even remember the first step now. Physiology was usually easier, and I thought that I had tackled a question from the extern on respiratory patterns in horses fairly well. I was beginning to feel that I was home and dry when the third examiner took over for his stint.

'Ah, good afternoon, Ms Hick,' declared the head as he introduced me to the extern. Although any other student would have been referred to as Miss Whoever, this particular lecturer persisted the whole year in pointedly addressing me as Ms Hick in supposed deference to my new marital status. 'Well, Ms Hick, I take if that you are familiar with avian anatomy?'

I gulped. Birds had never really featured strongly in my limited knowledge of physiology and apart from the fact that there was something funny about their lungs, they had lots of air in their bones and turkeys had green testicles, I didn't know much about them. I was fairly sure that not one of these gems of wisdom was what he had in mind.

'Ms Hick,' he continued, 'would you care, perhaps, to enlighten us in relation to the thermodynamic regulation of the feathered species?'

Not particularly, I thought to myself. 'Eh, well, if they get hot, they ... em ... pant ... or something,' I began nervously, beginning to feel a bit hot under the collar myself.

'Brilliant, Ms Hick,' he declared dryly. 'And would you care to expand?'

Frantically, I racked my brains trying to dredge up any other piece of information I might have in my scant array of avian knowledge. 'Well, em, they have this piece of tissue in their throats and if they get too hot they flap it and ...' I paused again, trying to remember why the hell they flapped it.

'Yes, Ms Hick?'

The silence seemed endless.

I continued haltingly: 'and ... the air passes over the tissue and that cools them down ... or something like that ...' I ended lamely, suddenly wondering if I was dreaming the whole thing or if it was really happening.

'Indeed, Ms Hick, and would you, perhaps, be familiar with the *term* for this mechanism?'

Silence again until inspiration hit me. Out of the depths of my mind came the term 'gullar flutter'. Yes, that was it, wasn't it ... or was it? Suddenly, I wasn't so sure.

'I presume you don't have any plans for the summer, Ms Hick?' This was always his way of letting you know you were going to fail and you would spend the holidays studying for repeats.

This is it, I thought to myself. Last chance. 'Yes, it's known as ...' my mind had gone blank. 'It's known as ...' I began again, slightly louder this time. Three sets of eyes boring into me: vultures waiting to swoop. 'It's known as ... gutter fucker!'

It took a few seconds for me to realise why the three suits were suddenly exploding into their handkerchiefs, trying to disguise the great guffaws of laughter that escaped as the tears streamed down their eyes.

That ended the oral but they passed me, probably for the sheer entertainment value I had inadvertently provided in an otherwise tedious day.

The summer of second year, I spent seeing practice with a variety of different vets and felt vaguely disappointed to find that really, although I enjoyed every call, I felt none the wiser in veterinary terms than I had felt in previous years before going to college at all!

Third year started more hopefully, with the introduction of microbiology, which would surely bring us closer to our final goal. By the end of the year, a lever-arch file was stuffed full of typed notes on the identification of the various bacteria, viruses, fungi and on all kinds of other bits of bacteriological knowledge that would hopefully enable us to earn a living in years to come. We first became acquainted with bacterial cultures in glass petri dishes in the labs and then in relation to the diseases they caused; this then led us on to the basic concepts of pathology. Pharmacology was in there too, but although this was supposed to enlighten us in relation to all aspects of the use of medicines and their mechanisms of action, and although we all supposedly passed the exam one way or another, I have a feeling that I wasn't the only one very busily reading the labels on the bottles when we eventually qualified.

It wasn't until fourth year, though, that we got into the thick of things clinical and spent the afternoons in the yard and in the consulting rooms. How chuffed we were with ourselves in our pristine overalls and spotless wellies, walking around the stable-yard, looking as though we were doing something important.

In the consulting rooms, we were finally given a case of our own. The unfortunate animal that arrived in for a routine booster vaccination was subjected to six novice vets, each vying with the other to carry out a clinical examination.

We were also allowed into theatre for the first time to watch the final-year students as they did their first neutering surgeries, under the supervision of the infinitely patient surgeons.

To give us a taste of being on call, we were all rostered on to the clinic for a day each term to stay until nine o'clock in the evening or whatever time was necessary for the particular cases in question. As luck would have it, while I was on, we had a spate of major liver surgeries in a litter of pedigree pups with a genetic disorder and so, instead of pottering around drinking cups of coffee and writing up the odd report, we each had to look after a critically ill animal. We were required to observe and note down all the vital signs such as temperature, heart rate, respiratory rate and a host of other parameters, every five minutes. As the junior, I was designated temperature, and dutifully recorded it at the prescribed intervals. In the warm recovery room, the two final-year students and I chatted to pass the time. We took it in turns to walk around the surgery to stretch our legs before returning to our posts. The rooms seemed eerie in the semi-light as the various monitors flickered and beeped, indicating that all was still well with the deeply sedated dog. Every half-hour or so, one of the vets would drop in to check on us.

Nothing much was happening and by half-past nine we were becoming stiff and bored. The conversation lulled as we lapsed into a silence broken only by the rhythmic bips of the monitors.

Suddenly, a shrill whistle erupted. We all jumped out of our semi-slumber, frantically trying to figure out from which machine the noise was coming. Although we had all been thoroughly drilled on the use of the equipment, this particular alarm call was unfamiliar to us. We double-checked our parameters. They all remained unchanged but still the sharp whistle continued at regular intervals. Quickly, one of the final years dialled the internal number to the vet's room. Within seconds, the sound of heavy foot-steps came from the corridors. In burst the senior surgeon and one of the anaesthetists to see what was going on.

As suddenly as it had begun, the panic was over, broken by the shriek of laughter from the anaesthetist. In a dark-ened corner of the room was a cage which contained another in-patient in the form of a Macaw parrot, a species famed for its skills of imitation. Although up to now, he had remained so silent that we had all but forgotten his presence, as the night was becoming dull, he had obviously decided to add in his own version of a monitor with a convincingly high-pitched whistle. As soon as he realised he had been sussed, he coyly hopped on one leg and hid his head under his wing.

Half an hour later, when the excitement had died down, he tried it again and was promptly removed. We laughed as his indignant shrieks faded as he was carried off to another, less critical unit.

As the summer of fourth year ended, it was hard to believe that next time around we would be out on our own, and we began final year with a mixture of elation and dread. Twenty-five short weeks to learn all we could know about veterinary medicine before being let loose on the general public, not to mention the unwitting animal population. As the weeks rushed by, a sense of desperation began to descend upon us and, before we knew it, we were heading into our final exams, still wondering when the moment of true enlightenment would dawn. A few weeks later, incredibly, the results table confirmed that we had passed. Now all that lay ahead was graduation day before we would be fully-fledged veterinary surgeons. By then it was beginning to dawn on us that, far from being over, our days of learning were only just beginning.

CHAPTER THREE

HORSE PRACTICE

B ut I had learned one thing already: the type of practice where I definitely did *not* want to work. One experience of horse practice was to influence my future choice of career options. In my final year at college, the thrill of seeing practice had become almost routine and, in common with my fellow students, I was torn between the desire to move on and get out on my own, and the worry of how I would actually perform once I was left to my own devices.

While out on calls with Finbar, he would let me do quite a bit of the practical work and I was beginning to feel that there was hope for me, not realising just how comfortable it was to have the safety net of an experienced vet on hand.

Although there were a lot of horses in his area, the work we did was confined to the basic, everyday jobs and any surgical cases would be referred to one of the specialist equine hospitals.

When a couple of flashy brochures appeared in the student common-room before the Easter holidays I was impressed. The glossy pictures of padded knock-down boxes and spacious stables, all occupied by impeccably groomed horses, looked appealing and gave us a taste for the posher end of things. One of the lecturers had a connection with a first-rate surgical referral hospital in Newmarket, in England, and promised to set me up there for a fortnight.

When I arrived at The Livingston Foundation Hospital, as the sign over the wrought-iron gates proudly proclaimed the place to be, I congratulated myself on my decision to go there. Such a grand-looking place must indeed be a veterinary hospital of academic excellence. I was equally impressed by the immaculate reception area where I announced my presence.

'You're who?' asked the haughty-looking woman behind the desk, peering at me over her spectacles.

'My name is Gillian Hick,' I repeated, slightly taken aback that nobody seemed to have heard of me. 'I'm here to see practice with Mr Livingston.'

'Oh, not another one!' she said dismissively. 'Well, go on over to the yard and just keep out of everyone's way until the vets arrive.'

Off I headed in my new Aigle boots and Gortex overalls, feeling somewhat crestfallen, but when I saw the magnificent red-bricked yard, filled with a collection of horses in varying stages of recovery from surgery, my spirits lifted. In the far corner was the surgical area and I looked in awe at the purpose-built, padded knock-down box, and separate theatre, filled with all sorts of sophisticated equipment that I had heard of, but never seen. As I wandered around the gleaming surgery, my experiences of rolling around mucky fields in pursuit of irate cattle with a few bales of straw serving as an operating table began to fade to a distant memory. I was just beginning to fancy myself working in a place like this when I heard a shout; 'Oi, you, what the hell do you think you're doing in there?'

I turned around to see a burly man, in jodhpurs embroidered with the hospital logo, and looked behind me to see who he was talking to.

'You!' he roared.

'Me?' I said, incredulously. 'Oh, I'm sorry, I didn't introduce myself. I'm the new veterinary student. My name is . . .'

My voice trailed off lamely as he roared 'I don't give a damn who you are! Just get out of there!'

Mortified, I came out of the surgery and stood in the middle of the yard, well aware that the small army of stable lads were having a good laugh at me. About half an hour passed as I stood there, trying to look engrossed at the pattern on the stable doors, until I finally got fed-up and cautiously made my way over to one of the more friendly-looking grooms who was busy mucking out.

'Can I give you a hand?' I enquired.

'Ta very much, love, but my life's worth more than that. The boss would kill me if I let you,' he said nodding over towards the man who had threatened to burst my eardrums.

'What time will the vets be along?' I enquired, wondering how long I could manage to stand around trying to look occupied.

'There's no surgery on today,' he replied. 'They've all gone off to the big race meeting. Mr Jeffers is on call but it would take something serious to bring him back. He's fond of the old you-know-what.'

'So what am I meant to do all day?' I asked him in despair.

'Beats me, luv!' He shrugged and turned away before the boss's beady eyes picked up on the conversation.

The day lasted a lifetime as I wandered around the yard afraid to look at, let alone touch, anything. At lunch time, the yard lads went off to their private quarters and left me standing there with the packed lunch that I had hurriedly bought at a local shop that morning. By six o'clock I was just about to leave, to make my way back to the tiny room in the B&B that I was staying in, when an impressive-looking Jaguar pulled into the car-park reserved for members of staff. One of the lads nudged me: 'That's Mr Livingston himself.'

Right, I thought to myself. I've had enough of this.

'Good evening, Mr Livingston,' I began, marching confidently across the yard. 'My name is Gillian Hick. I'm a veterinary student from Ireland and I wonder would it be possible for me to work with you tomorrow?'

Mr Livingston was a portly man, in late middle-age, with a brisk demeanour. He eyeballed me over his heavy spectacles and, looking disdainfully at the hand I held out to him, he muttered, 'I'm afraid not. I'll be leaving the yard at 6.30am. I've a call to attend to on the far side of town.'

'That's perfect,' I replied, determined not to give up. 'I'll see you here at 6.30am so.'

I was aware of a silence behind me as the group of lads stood watching in anticipation.

'Don't be late, then,' he said testily, before he marched off to his office, shutting the door firmly behind him.

'Good for you!' said the only one of the lads who had talked to me yet.

By 6.25am the next morning, I was waiting at the yard entrance for Mr Livingston; 6.30am came and went and then 7.30 and then 7.45. Had it not been for the well-meaning lecturer in college who had organised the job for me, I would have packed up and caught the next flight home.

At exactly 7.48, I heard the smooth roar of the approaching Jag. Mr Livingston looked surprised to see me as I approached the car.

'Yes, well, I'm a few minutes late,' he said, without looking at me.

'Not to worry,' I replied sweetly. 'I'm sure you're a very busy man.'

He was so engrossed in his own self-importance that he failed to notice my sarcasm.

'That's right, indeed. Very busy,' he affirmed.

I had barely shut the car door before Mr Livingston had taken off and, with the radio blaring at full blast, I was left in no doubt that having to make polite conversation was not going to be an issue. Four years of seeing practice with an assortment of vets had left me accustomed to dealing with all types of characters. I sat back and allowed my mind to wander as the car shot along the motorway to the town where the first call was to be. After a while though, my reveries were interrupted by hunger pangs. Vets in general seem to be a hungry lot and part of the ritual of seeing practice usually involved regularly stopping off for supplies at the local shops or pubs, so much so that my metabolism became accustomed to the increased food intake during these regular 'working holidays'. By the time ten o'clock approached, I was ravenous. The two packets of Hula-Hoops that I had eaten for breakfast were now a distant memory and I knew I wouldn't survive much longer. The only thing that gave me hope was the sight of the gut protruding over Mr Livingston's belt; judging by its ample size, I figured that he wouldn't last long either. I was right.

Not long after, he pulled into one of the roadside cafés and as I watched him pile up a bag from the hot-food counter, I felt relieved at the prospect of food, at last.

But I was in for a rude awakening. When he returned to the car, he got back into his seat and carefully pulled out a breakfast roll, two hot doughnuts and settled a steaming cup of coffee on the dashboard. He then proceeded to wolf it all down without even a sideways glance at me. My total sense of outrage was subdued only by the fact that I was almost weak with hunger at this stage. As we travelled the last few miles to the yard where the lame horse awaited, I fumed at his ignorance. Never in all my years of seeing practice had I encountered a vet as rude as this. It was an unwritten rule among colleagues to look after students – after all, they had all been students themselves once.

I have little memory of the actual call itself. All I could

think about was that my feet were going numb while the feisty little yearling trotted up and down as Mr Livingston tried to make up his mind what was wrong with her.

When we finally got back to the hospital, my only thought was for the humble sandwich that I had packed in case of emergency. By the time I had finished it, Mr Livingston had gone and so another day had ended.

Soon, I was actually beginning to wonder about my career choice. My experiences since arriving at this place had been so disheartening that, for the first time ever, I felt I was beginning to hate the veterinary world. In any other practice that I had worked in, the vets were delighted if you showed an interest in a case, once you didn't pester them too much about it. Here, there was an air of secrecy over everything and I soon found that the case-files that I normally enjoyed poring over in my spare moments, were jealously guarded. I wasn't allowed to handle any of the animals and the vets' meeting that took place twice a week was held behind closed doors. When the vets went to the staff-room for a cup of coffee, the door was kept firmly shut so I was left in no doubt that my presence was not welcome. My sole form of refreshment was from the water-hose out in the yard.

* * *

One day, one of the vets finally took pity on me and allowed me to watch a colic surgery from such a distance that all I could see was the sterile, green drape. Another day, he took me out to X-ray a horse in one of the top racing yards – I was supposed to be suitably impressed by the name of the yard, but in truth I had never heard of it, owing to my ignorance of the racing scene.

The yard itself was more interesting than the X-ray procedure. I had never before seen so many rows of boxes with so many sleek racehorses. I arrived just as what was known as a changeover was taking place; the first string of horses was being unloaded from one fleet of lorries while the next were getting ready to go. The lorries were headed for the gallops where twenty or so apprentice jockeys would put the horses through their paces, under the supervision of the head jockey. What amazed me was the average age of these jockeys; some of them didn't look old enough to be out of national school.

'Stop snivelling and get your horse loaded!' shrilled the trainer.

The poor kid to whom she referred was a tiny little spotty-faced lad, no more than four feet tall, who had apparently taken a bad fall that morning and was trying to swap his somewhat excitable mount for one of the others.

All my romantic views of working in a racing yard faded in the half hour I spent there in an increasingly tense atmosphere while the trainer stalked around, barking out orders to each jockey in relation to their mount. They were all clearly terrified of her although, as soon as she left, the camaraderie between them became evident.

I only saw Mr Livingston once more, on the Thursday morning when he came in to do a fairly routine surgery list. One bay mare was written up to be pin-fired – an old fashioned treatment for tendon injuries in which red hot needles are inserted at regular intervals along the damaged tendon in an attempt to set up a counter-irritation to promote better healing of the affected area. Although the procedure is carried out under local anaesthetic, the after-effects are quite painful and the benefit of the treatment doubtful. I was surprised to see such an old-fashioned treatment still in use in a modern hospital but even more surprised when I managed to sneak a look at the horse when no one was looking. I ran my hand down along the mare's leg and could easily identify the deep and superficial flexor tendons but, no matter how hard I tried, I couldn't find even the slightest blemish in either. When Mr Livingston arrived to examine her, despite being strongly discouraged by the vets from asking questions, I decided to risk it.

'What are you planning on doing with her?' I asked him, feigning innocence.

'Pin-firing,' came the abrupt reply.

'And why are you doing that?' I continued, despite his discouraging manner.

'Well now,' he said, in the longest sentence he had yet spoken to me, 'if you can't see why she needs to be pin-fired, it only confirms that you're in the wrong job.'

Despite several more examinations, I still couldn't figure out why she needed to be pin-fired.

By Friday morning, I couldn't believe that I was only halfway through my stay. While on the phone to Donal the previous night, he had encouraged me to come home early. 'By the sounds of things, they won't even notice over there,' he pointed out. But I just couldn't face leaving early to hear the slagging I'd get back home about the abrupt ending to my high-flying career plans as a horse vet. If this was equine veterinary, I didn't want to know about it.

The day passed as usual, hanging around hoping to catch a glimpse of something vaguely interesting, and at the same time, trying to keep a low profile, since any effort I made to lend a hand or get involved was always rebuffed.

As usual, lunchtime found me sitting on a bale of straw, having a sandwich with the yard dog for company. My peaceful daydreams were interrupted by the roar of a lorry careering around the corner. I quickly recognised it as belonging to the trainer in the yard where we had gone to X-ray a horse. Apparently, she would often get it into her head that a particular horse needed to be endoscoped after the morning training session and she would arrive without appointment and expect the job to be done instantly. Although no other client would have been let away with this, as she was such a prestigious trainer the vets would fawn over her in a way that made me want to cringe every time she came into the yard. Within seconds of the lorry screeching to a halt, a flurry of jockeys piled out of the back and began unloading horses. As I made my way across the yard to see if I could give a hand, she caught sight of me.

'Girl. You. Stop idling in the corner and get a box ready for the horse. Chop, chop!' she said, clapping her hands at me.

Suddenly, the long hours of standing around being ignored got to me, as did the ongoing pangs of hunger, and the looks of contempt that the vets threw at me every time I was lucky enough for one of them to notice me. The temper I had been keeping in check all week began to boil over.

'Chop, chop, I said!' she commanded imperiously.

The temper erupted. 'I have a name, and for your information it's Gillian. I'm not an employee of the hospital and, thankfully, I'm not an employee of yours either, so why don't you go get one of your own slaves to do it for you?' I said in as cool and collected a voice as I could muster. I then calmly walked out of the place, desperately conscious of the stunned silence from her yard lads who had probably never before seen her gaping like a wounded goldfish.

Needless to say, I didn't come back the next week, or ever again for that matter. My only reminder of that long, miserable week now is on the odd occasion when that trainer appears on some racing programme or other and I point her out to Donal as my only connection to the racing world!

It was a bit awkward back in college after the holiday when my lecturer asked me how I had got on, but when I gave him a slightly edited account of the events he just laughed and said that I must have been spoiled by the other vets I saw practice with. He was probably right, but I wasn't complaining. At least it did one thing for me: when we finally qualified, I steered well clear of the jobs with the glossy brochures.

I discovered, on comparing notes with my classmates, that most of them had experienced nothing but genuine hospitality at the other English equine hospitals and there was even a story of one of the lads being allowed to do half a colic surgery, although we never quite believed that one. I felt that I had indeed been unlucky and hard done by. For all the effort and expense of going there I had acquired practically no valuable experience of any kind.

It was unfortunate that my stint in that yard was my last experience of seeing practice because, up until then, I had thoroughly enjoyed the life as a carefree observer. It definitely steered me away from the 'posher' jobs when, three months later, I went looking for my first job, although as I soon discovered, animals in all walks of life have one thing in common – their total unpredictability. And that is matched only by the unpredictability of their owners, no matter what their accent.

What lay ahead when I left the protective cocoon of the veterinary college on graduation day, clutching an innocuous-looking scroll of paper, was a steep learning curve as a veterinary surgeon. Soon I would have to contend, on my own, with animals who refused to read the textbooks, and with owners who ranged from the saintly to the bizarre. A whole new life was about to begin.

INNER-CITY PRACTICE

CHAPTER FOUR

MY FIRST PATIENT

The Monday morning after graduation day saw me making my way over the toll-bridge and around Dublin's inner city, to begin my first job. I had spent the previous months, while supposedly busy studying for finals, scanning the college noticeboard for job ads. In anticipation of a nice job and a new life, Donal and I had spent many hours driving around looking at houses. As he had long since had his own butcher's shop in Dalkey, we were confined to Wicklow in our search, but that was no disadvantage. I sort of fancied myself in a nice mixed-animal practice, with lots of experienced vets on hand, some qualified nurses and all the paraphernalia of X-ray machines, scanners and blood-testing machines, the likes of which would be found in any modern, progressive practice.

While waiting for 'the perfect job', I got a call from a friend who had once worked in a practice with two other vets, Michael, the boss, and Justin, now two years out of college. Seemingly, Michael had broken his leg while out testing cattle and was going to be out of action for the next few months.

'They're really stuck,' pleaded my friend, 'and Justin is a dead sound guy.'

It turned out that the practice covered mainly the companion animals of the inner city, along with whatever horses were still around, and also included occasional forays outside the city. At least the job would allow me to work from home, although it would involve a lot of driving,

'Well, does he want me to go out for an interview or something?' I asked, playing for time.

'No!' my friend was emphatic. 'Just turn up on Monday morning.'

I pulled into the little yard at the side of the surgery, with a grimy Barna shed behind it. It wasn't really what I had expected.

It didn't take long for Justin to give me a guided tour of the premises. I couldn't help noticing that the floor of the tiny waiting-room, with its half-dozen chairs, was strewn with assorted animal hair. The consulting room, which doubled as a theatre, wasn't much bigger and it led on out to a series of metal cages, in need of a fresh coat of paint, which served as a kennelling area.

Justin's companions in the practice consisted of Liz, a pleasant sixteen-year-old who had progressed from working on Saturday mornings to leaving school and coming to work full time, and Popeye, an ancient looking, one-eyed cat who apparently had come with the premises when the practice had opened some twelve years previously.

'Listen, sorry to leave you like this,' began Justin, as Liz pushed a mug of lukewarm coffee into my hand, 'but I have to go out on a call – there's a foal caught up in wire in one of the old dumps. God knows how long it's been there. Are you okay on your own?'

I nodded bravely, despite my feeling of trepidation at being abandoned, but as the only consultation booked in so far was a routine kitten vaccination, I could hardly object.

Although it took me almost twenty minutes, I was delighted with myself when the kitten went off, duly vaccinated with the correct vaccination, which I had found after a bit of rummaging through the tiny fridge that held the supplies.

Liz was on the phone as I came back in after seeing the client out.

'There's a Mr Molloy on his way in with a sick dog,' she said to me as she hung up. 'Says she's in a bad way.'

'Oh right,' I replied, trying to sound casual. 'Did he say what was wrong with her?'

'Just that she's been vomiting for a while and now she won't get up.'

I mentally ran through a haphazard list of diagnoses of vomiting, collapsed dogs. 'Did Justin say what time he'd be back at?'

'No. I'd say he'll be a while, though. It'll take him an age to get across the city.'

I didn't have much more time to worry about it before the tinkling bell announced the client and Liz ushered him into the consulting room with his dog. I couldn't help thinking what an ugly little dog it was. The short, twisted legs, each one pointing in a different direction, were barely able to support the long, broad body. It was impossible to make out what the original colour of the coat had been but it was now a dirty grey and stuck in long, tangled mats to the animal's emaciated frame. Two ears were plastered to her neck and the oddly-shaped tail drooped between her hind legs. Her eyes were glazed as she lay there, resigned to her fate. I was so shocked by the condition of the dog that I instantly forgot my own apprehension. My initial impression was that this dog was dying, beyond any help that the intervention of a novice vet could provide.

'She's in a really bad way, Mr Molloy,' I said coldly to the owner.

He became instantly defensive. 'Well, I can tell ye this now, Doctor,' he began. 'She was right as rain up until this morning. Ye wouldn't believe how quickly she went down.'

Despite my inexperience, I didn't.

As I stretched out my hand and rubbed along the collapsed body on the consulting table, I couldn't help noticing the numerous scars hidden in the ragged coat. The dog warningly bared her teeth at me, although somehow I felt that she was not an aggressive type.

Ignoring my silence, Mr Molloy continued: 'When I got up this morning she'd been sick all over the box. She won't eat for me now and there's an awful stink off her.'

My worst fears were confirmed as a putrid discharge

dripped from the little dog's vagina onto the stainless steel surface of the table. I didn't need much experience to make my diagnosis.

'Has she been drinking much lately?' I enquired.

'Well, I gave her a drink yesterday morning and she drank that all right.'

'But surely she's had water since then?'

'Ah well, now, I can't leave the water in with her. She'd only knock it over on herself.'

'Is she not out at all during the day?'

'Well, she was mated last week and I don't want another dog to get in at her, but she's in a fine big box,' he said indicating a space approximately two foot by three, barely big enough for the dog to fit into.

As I examined the deep purple mucous membranes of her gums, I noticed that all her front teeth had been worn away, presumably from trying to gnaw her way out of her container. I suspected it might have been her home for a lot longer than two weeks. A warning bell began to ring in my mind.

'Have you ever bred from her before?'

'I have indeed. Sure, she's never missed a heat since she was six months old. I normally cross her with a Glen of Imaal like herself, but this time I decided to try her with a Kerry Blue. She took a good covering so I hope the pups will be okay.'

Everything fell into place. The Glen of Imaal was an uncommon but highly-valued breed – easy to sell for good cash. It was not unusual for them to be crossed with a Kerry Blue, which yielded a tough, aggressive dog, perfect for the illegal sport of dog-fighting. I wasn't surprised by her reaction to me now. I suspected that this dog had endured a life of intensive puppy-breeding and dog fights.

'Did she have many pups in her previous litters?' I asked, barely able to control my rising temper although I knew I had to. If this man thought for one minute that I would go against him, the little bitch would be taken away and I would never see her again. Looking at her present condition, I reckoned she would be dead by that evening without treatment. I had come across a few cases of pyometra when seeing practice and understood the pathology of the condition: the infection that builds up in the uterus, resulting in a life-threatening septicaemia. But I had never seen an affected animal as sick as this dog.

'Well, she had a good few pups before but the last two litters died. I had to go away for the weekend but I left her a good sup of water an' all and some food in the box. I'll tell ye, though, she's not a great mother 'cos when I came back each time, they were all dead. But I'll watch her like a hawk this time. I have a few orders for those pups already. D'ye think she has many in her?'

'She's not in pup, Mr Molloy. She has an infection in her womb. Just look at the discharge from her. We'll be very lucky to save her.'

'Damn!' he said shaking his head in despair. 'I've had nothing but bad luck with this bitch. I don't know if she's worth going on with. Is it going to cost me much? I'm not a wealthy man, ye know.'

Looking down at the panting dog on the table, I wondered if it would be kinder to end it all for her, here and now, and yet she had the look of a tough dog about her. I just didn't have enough experience to know if she could pull through or not. Anyway, it seemed a shame to give up on her now. I vowed there and then that she would not be going back to her owner no matter what happened, but I would have to play it carefully. Animal welfare issues in this country are still very poorly defined and it's notoriously difficult to get a prosecution of any sort. The law was not on my side and Mr Molloy looked to be every bit as tough as his dog.

'The cost will depend on what we have to do with her. We'll have to keep her in overnight at least. She needs to go on a drip and she also needs some intensive antibiotic therapy. We'll have a better idea by tomorrow.'

'Well, I don't want to end up with a big bill for a useless bitch. Ye won't go too hard on me, will ye?' he said, winking at me slyly.

I ignored his question and called for Liz to take the little dog to the treatment area.

'If you'll just fill in an admission form, please, then we can get to work on her.'

In rough letters, he filled in the section for name and address without hesitation. He left a blank for the dog's details and vaccination history.

'All my dogs are good an' healthy,' he said, indicating the blank space. 'They don't need any of that rubbish.' He signed the consent form and without a backward glance, made for the door.

'Excuse me, Mr Molloy. What's her name?' I called after him.

'Em … ' He turned back for a moment. 'Jess.'

More like Brood Bitch Number Six, I thought to myself.

I tried ringing Justin on his mobile but he must have been out of cover and I knew we had no time to waste. With the help of Liz, I set up a drip to rehydrate our new patient and flush out the toxins that had built up in her system. I added in some intravenous antibiotics and the strongest possible drug I could find to reduce her raging temperature. I also injected her with an anti-emetic to stop the continuous vomiting. Having looked through the cupboards at the limited assortment of drugs, I made up a solution of antiseptic and antibiotic, which I flushed into her womb, by means of a long catheter.

'Might be worth giving the welfare group a call to see if they can trace yer man,' suggested Liz, as I adjusted the drip to what I hoped would be the correct flow rate of fluids.

She dialled the number for me and, having introduced myself to the inspector, I told him the story. I read out the address on the form which my client had filled in.

'Well, we'll certainly follow it up,' he replied, 'but chances are it's a false address. We may never be able to trace him.'

By the time Justin had returned, my first in-patient seemed to be a little brighter, but he was doubtful.

'Did you get any money from him?' he asked me. I had to admit that it hadn't even occurred to me to try.

The rest of the day passed with what, in time, would become routine consultations for me, but the thrill of being let loose on the surgery was dimmed slightly by my anxiety about the fate of the helpless dog.

As I was new to the job, Justin told me that Michael, the boss who was out sick, had asked him to cover nights for the first week to give me a chance to break myself in gently.

'What are we going to do with the dog?' he asked me once the afternoon rush was over. 'I wonder should we hand her over to the welfare group?' he continued without waiting for me to reply. 'I doubt if that Molloy fellow will come back for her and, even if he does, if we find out that he has given us a false address, he won't have a leg to stand on.'

'What will happen her then?' I asked.

'Well, to be honest, they'll probably put her to sleep. She's so sick that her chances of making it are slim and if she has been used as a fighting dog, well, she's not going to have the temperament to be re-homed, even if she does make it.'

I was in a quandary. The thought of abandoning the dog, who had already been through so much, seemed terrible but, equally, it was Justin's time, as he was the one who would have to tend to her through the night, and the practice's money that I would be wasting.

'Well, what about if I take her home with me and see how she is in the morning?' I asked, thinking aloud.

Justin shrugged his shoulders. 'Fine by me. Just don't get your hopes up.'

Back home, I had to leave all the car doors open to get rid of the stench that still lingered even after I had taken the little dog out. Donal, having arrived home long before me, had prepared a celebratory dinner for my first working day.

'Who's the dog?' he asked, looking slightly surprised as I carried in the lifeless form.

'It's a long story!' I said, and then explained the day's events.

He didn't seem too put out but casually asked, 'And is it normal to have to take a patient home?'

'Oh God no!' I replied confidently. 'It'll probably never happen again … and it's only for tonight.'

He said nothing, in his wisdom, realising, more than I, that this would be the first of many.

I settled the little dog down on an old duvet in the small utility room, with her drip suspended from a hook on the window ledge. Our two dogs, Spook, a black Labrador, and Judy, a yellow one, seemed quite pleased by the new addition to the family and sniffed her over inquisitively even though the dog seemed oblivious to their presence.

Throughout the night, I constantly adjusted her fluids and repeated her injections, and the next morning I flushed her uterus again. By then, she was at least making an effort to move. I noticed that her joints seemed to be painful and that she made no attempt to rise but dragged herself around on her belly, struggling to pull herself along with her two front legs while her two hind legs stretched out behind. I couldn't help thinking that she looked just like a giant slug.

She growled warningly at me as I manipulated her crooked joints trying to ascertain whether her failure to rise was due the condition of her joints or just from generalised weakness. I found they were stiff and arthritic even though Mr Molloy has said that she was only three years old. The supporting musculature had all but wasted away. I supposed it was from a combination of inbreeding, poor feeding and prolonged, forced confinement. I wondered just how long she had lived in that box.

Justin and Liz were both surprised when I carried my patient back into work later that morning. I think they thought I was being a bit optimistic. As the day went on, she did seem to be improving, although she refused to eat and was still vomiting occasionally, despite the anti-emetics.

'Doesn't she look just like a big slug?' I laughed to Liz, as the dog tried to drag herself across the kennel floor, for the first time taking an interest in the ginger tom across the way from her.

'I think you've just hit on the name for her. It suits her more than Jess.'

I held my breath every time the doorbell rang, expecting to see Mr Molloy, but he never showed up.

The inspector called from the welfare office. 'Bad news, I'm afraid; another false address. There's no such place.'

I cursed under my breath. 'Thanks for trying anyway,' I replied wearily. 'I'll let you know if we hear any more from him.'

'What do you want to do with her now?' enquired Justin as by four o'clock that afternoon there was still no contact from her owner.

'Well, she's doing much better now. Her temperature is back to normal and the discharge has almost stopped.'

'Well, that's great,' he assured me, 'but she still needs to be spayed and we can't do that unless the owner pays for it.'

Although I was in a precarious position as a newly-qualified, newly-appointed assistant, I couldn't bear to give up on my first real patient now. I said nothing, refusing to suggest what really was the only sensible option.

'Well, you do what you like, then,' said Justin finally, obviously irritated by my novice's attitude to abandoned dogs. 'But if anything comes of it you can explain to Michael what happened.'

'Oh! Hi dog!' said Donal as we came in the door that evening. 'I though you were only here for one night.' He laughed as I tried to explain. 'It's all right. I didn't believe you anyway – even if *you* did!'

That night, we had a long-standing arrangement to go to the local barn dance with two friends we hadn't met for a few months. I couldn't back out at this late stage as they had travelled some distance to get there. Slug lay peacefully by the fire, having decided it was more cosy than the utility room. Spook and Judy took up their usual positions, entwined in a black and yellow ball on an old armchair.

'Look after the patient,' I told them and laughed as Spook wagged her tail in acknowledgement while Judy didn't even miss a snore. We hoped to be back in an hour or two. I should have known better. I began to unwind after the first drink, and, despite the pressures of the day, I ended up having a good time. Slug seemed a bit bemused by my joviality when I returned and kept up her usual growling as I gently flushed and injected her. I really didn't think that her constant snarling was due to anything other than her past ill-treatment. I was sure that if she pulled through, she would come around with a little bit of kindness and that I could then find a suitable home for her.

Before I went to bed, I set the alarm for six the next morning. It wasn't until I was woken by the persistent ringing that I realised that long working hours and late nights don't mix. As I flushed out her uterus again, the smell from her persistent discharge assailed my tender nostrils. Before long, both Slug and I were vomiting in the back garden. For the first time she turned and wagged her tail at me. I think she thought I was going out in sympathy.

I had recovered sufficiently by the time I got to work. But shortly after 11.00am my heart froze as I recognised Mr Molloy's voice in the waiting room. Slug lay patiently in the kennels next door.

'How's my little bitch, then?'

'She's still very sick, I'm afraid. We'll have to keep in her for longer.'

'Well, I dunno about that. I think I'll just take her home with me. If yer jabs haven't fixed her by now, there's not much chance. Can I have a look at her?'

'I'm afraid that's not possible. She's not here at the moment,' I lied nervously. 'She's in our intensive care unit. She can't leave until she's a lot better and we don't allow visitors.'

I looked in alarm as his eyes narrowed and his face reddened. 'That's a bloody good bitch of mine, that is! I won't have ye messing around with her.'

'Of course not, that's why she needs such intensive

treatment. Now, if you don't mind, we'll also need some payment to cover the cost of the treatment so far.' I didn't care in the slightest about the money but I thought it might get rid of him.

'Well, I've nothing on me now. Ye'll have to wait. How much is the bill anyway?'

I took out a sheet of headed paper and carefully started doing a breakdown of the costs. I thought of every single injection, every flush, every millilitre of fluids, every mile I had driven her, every hour I had worked with her and I wrote them all down. For each item, I picked a figure and then carefully totted them all up.

'So you see, Mr Molloy, the bill at the moment stands at three hundred and fifty-eight euro, plus VAT,' I replied calmly, hoping my voice wouldn't shake. I had to get the bill up to more than what he could sell her for. I was sure that was his only interest in her.

'What?! That's bloody ridiculous!' he exclaimed, going from red to purple. For a moment I thought he was going to have a heart attack.

'Well, unfortunately, that's not all. If she were to come in heat again the infection would recur so she'll have to be spayed as well. That will cost another hundred and fifty euro or so.' It would also significantly reduce her resale value if she was spayed. 'We'll need the money by tomorrow.'

'This is crazy. I'll have to think about it,' he muttered faintly. Obviously he had done the same rough calculations as I had. He would be lucky to get a couple of hundred euro for her, even if she had papers.

'Take all the time you like,' I replied calmly. 'Drop in tomorrow and let us know. Of course, if you decide it's not worth bothering with, you'll still owe us the three hundred and fifty-eight euro, plus an extra forty for putting her to sleep. Plus VAT.'

He walked out, muttering in disgust. I felt I had won the battle.

That evening, Slug picked a piece of fresh chicken out of my hand although she never took her wary eyes off me. She came on in leaps and bounds after that. I never saw Mr Molloy again but it took a long time before my heart didn't stop every time the doorbell rang. After ten days, with no further contact from the owner, Justin decided that she had been officially abandoned and, with a bit of persuasion, agreed to spay her as there was no way I was going to do it myself so early in my surgical career.

I was right in my early assessment: with a bit of time and patience, Slug became a very friendly dog. I was wrong, though, in thinking that I would find a nice home for her; Slug picked me.

As the days went by and we travelled in and out to work together, she became increasingly devoted to me. I got used to my little shadow and she would often lie unnoticed at my feet as I consulted or carried out operations. I eventually gave up telling Donal every day that she would be going soon – and he had long since given up listening anyway! Gradually, her health improved and before long she was unrecognisable. Her ears now point upwards, her coat is glossy and only the crooked legs remain as a testimony to those early days of ill-treatment. After the five months, when Michael returned to work and I left to find my next job, Slug came with me. I couldn't imagine life without her now and I laugh when I remember that my initial reaction to her was 'What an ugly dog'. How very wrong I was!

CHAPTER FIVE

GETTING STUCK IN

I paused, and closed my fingers around the large, soft mass at the angle of the horse's jaw. With an air of brave decisiveness that I certainly didn't feel, I plunged the sharpened blade deep into the softest point and jumped sideways as an arc of bloody pus spewed out of my incision.

An enthusiastic roar from the assembled onlookers, with exclamations of 'Jaysus, Missus, ye'll bleedin' kill 'im!' and 'I think I'm gonna puke!' rewarded my efforts, as the crowd scattered to avoid the discharge which had by now reduced to a trickle. I gently massaged the area with a swab to ensure that the last of the discharge had drained. An abscess is not uncommon in a horse and in most cases poses no great threat to the animal. In this case, however, it was located in the deadliest of positions, between a maze of major nerves and arteries; the slightest slip of the blade and I would have been making arrangements to have the body taken away.

The piebald shook himself and looked around as though wondering what all the fuss was about. Bursting the abscess had brought about instant relief from pain and he happily lowered his head to pick at the grass.

I was delighted with myself to have brought about such a spectacular improvement with a minimum of input. If it hadn't been for the fact that Justin was already out calving a cow when this call had come in, I undoubtedly would have shied away from going out to what had sounded like a very sick horse.

Johnny, the sixteen-year old who owned the piebald, turned to me with an earnest look on his face. 'Thanks very much, Missus! Me Da gave me Charlo de nigh' before 'e was kilt. 'E means a lot te me, 'e does.'

Johnny's father had been found dead one night, in the rough waste ground at the back of the estate, in what was probably a drugs-related crime.

As we walked back across the fields, I noted with relief that my car was still where I had left it and nothing appeared to have been tampered with. During my first week in the practice, I had spent over an hour in a neighbouring estate, painstakingly stitching a horse that had got caught on the railway line, only to be rewarded by finding my car-radio ripped out. Justin was sympathetic, but warned me that if I got the name of being a soft touch in the area, I wouldn't last long. With this in mind, I had left Johnny's older brother minding the car with the threat that if anything was missing on my return, they could find another vet to do their work. All was in order.

I was surprised when Johnny pulled a wad of tattered

twenty-euro banknotes out of his back pocket. 'How much, Missus?' He paid me the sixty euro and I went on my way.

I left clear instructions about how to bathe and clean the wound and I didn't expect to hear any more from them. So I was surprised to see young Johnny sitting outside the surgery wall that evening, carrying a bulky-looking parcel, carelessly wrapped in rough brown paper.

'How's Charlo doing?' I called out, trying not to sound alarmed.

He smile broadly. 'Shur, he's aytin' everythin' dat's put in front of 'im. He must 'ave been half-starved with all de poison in 'is blood. Paddy on the green said he'd 'ave been in de knackers' yard by now if ye hadn't come out.' With that, he dropped the parcel into my hands and then quickly disappeared around the corner without looking back.

I was bewildered, not to say a little alarmed, as to what the contents of the parcel might be, but I didn't get a chance to have a look until later on in the evening, when the rush at the surgery had calmed to a manageable level. Cautiously, I put my hand in the bag and gasped in horror when I realised what it was: a brand new car-radio, freshly ripped out of some other unfortunate's car, wires still attached. The neighbours in inner-city estates had a great sense of loyalty to their own. Clearly, Johnny's gang now considered me one of theirs. I found myself in a total quandary. While I didn't want to accept stolen property, neither did I want to offend Johnny's sense of loyalty – however misguided. Either way, it was highly unlikely that the owner of this car-radio, among the dozens that would have been stolen that day, would ever be reunited with his or her property. Hurriedly, I stuffed the radio back in its bag and hid it among a pile of junk in a drawer in the surgery. But one problem still remained: how would I ever explain today's returns in the first meeting scheduled with the accountant next week? And what was the VAT rate on payment by means of stolen car radios?

CHAPTER SIX

BRUNO'S
LAST HOURS

'We have yer man in the van, luv,' said the man who had just appeared on the doorstep of the surgery.

'Will ye do 'im in for us?' added his companion.

I gulped, trying not to appear too taken aback. Looking at the pair of them, I suddenly wished I hadn't arrived in early, before either Liz or Justin.

'Yer man?' I repeated nervously.

'Yeah, yer man I was tellin' ye about last night on the phone.'

'Oh, of course, the old dog,' I replied, as the memory of the bizarre phone call I had received some hours previously came flooding back.

I had been in a deep sleep when the phone had rung, and I paused just long enough to glance at the clock before pressing the answer button: the digital light flashed 4.38am.

As I held the phone to my ear, all I could hear was loud, thumping, heavy-metal music and the sounds of a party in full swing. Please, please, I thought to myself, let it be a wrong number.

'Is tha' de doctor?' roared a suspiciously high-sounding voice over the background din.

'Yes,' I replied, by now getting used to my honorary status. 'What can I do for you?' I continued as abruptly as possible in my state of semi-slumber, anticipating a long story.

And a long story it was.

Ten minutes later, I was still being regaled with the story of a stray dog who had been adopted by the local community and now, at sixteen years of age, they decided it was time to have him put to sleep — at 4.38 in the morning.

At least three voices were enthusiastically filling me in on all the sordid details.

'He's been around since I got me first moped, Missus. An' ye wouldn't wanna see de poor aul' brute sufferin', like.'

'An' we 'ave the money an all, we had a bit of a whip around for 'im there tonight. So dere's no problem with tha' end a things.'

'It's just that,' the initial spokesman was back, a slight catch in his voice this time, 'he's like a son to me ...' and the voice trailed off.

'Ah Jaysus, would ye give us back de phone, Gerry, ye girl's blouse ye! Will ye do it for us, Doc? Will ye do 'im in for us?'

'You say he's sixteen years old, but is he in a lot of pain or anything?'

'Ah no, love, it's just that the auld legs are goin' on 'im and he's pissin' on 'imself an' there isn't a pick on 'im.'

'Well, it certainly sounds like his quality of life is gone,' I began, trying to sound sympathetic, 'but I don't really see that he needs to be put to sleep *right now*.'

'Ah Jaysus, no love! Sure we don't even know where de fecker is. Goes off wanderin' after birds at night 'e does. Still a bit of a boyo – although I don't think 'e could get de leg over now,' he added with a bawdy laugh.

'Naw, me and the lads was just 'aving a few joints and we got talkin' and we just wanned to know if ye'd do de job for us. Shur, ye couldn't come out now, luv – it's after four in the morning, ye know,' he added, sounding a bit concerned about my state of consciousness.

'What was all that about?' asked Donal blearily as I put the phone down. He looked at me disbelievingly as I filled him in. 'You do have some strange clients!' was his only comment before sinking back into the pillows.

The next morning, I had a vague recollection of the conversation, but as this was mixed together with my later dreams of aged Collies smoking joints while roaring round the local estates on motorbikes, I wasn't quite sure what was fact and what was fiction.

'Will ye come an' have a look at Bruno? See what ye think?'

I followed the pair out to the back of the van and there, on a well-worn but comfortable blanket, lay your typical 'street dog'. No fancy collars or name tags adorned the shaggy neck. He was a mongrel – a remote pure-blooded ancestor had doubtlessly had his wicked way with some unknown mate of indeterminate breed, probably late one night in a dark alleyway. His thick, matted coat had faded from what had once been a glossy black to a dull, reddish brown.

'Come on, Bruno, let's have a look at you,' I coaxed.

He thumped his tail good-naturedly as I hoisted him up. He didn't object as I ran my hands over him, noting the wasted muscles of his hind-quarters and the smelly, soiled coat – a sure sign of his incontinence. As I pulled out my stethoscope to listen to the rhythmic swishing of what had once been a healthy heart, he coughed deeply as though to confirm my diagnosis.

'Yes,' I said thoughtfully, turning to face the two men. 'He's had a long life but he's come to the end of the road now. Do you want to bring him on into the surgery?'

'Ah no way. Shur, de lads would kill us if we didn't bring 'im back. We just brought 'im out to see what ye thought. Will ye come back to the house with us and do it? All de lads are waiting.'

No amount of persuading would convince them it made much more sense for me to do the job there and then. Somehow, this old dog had gone from being a stray, surviving on the occasional scraps thrown out to him, to enjoying the status of a revered pet who had now come to the end of the line and required a home death and burial – and, by the sound of things, a wake.

Reluctantly, I gathered my clippers, syringes and a bottle of the pleasantly pink-tinted lethal injection.

It wasn't until I was following them out across the city that my thoughts began to turn to the task ahead. Although

at this stage I had amassed a vast sixteen weeks' experience as a practising vet, I had never yet had to put an
animal to sleep.

In college, we had often discussed how awful it must to
have to do it with an owner present. 'Relax,' said one of
the students dismissively. 'Sure, how could it go wrong?
It's not as if you can make a balls of it. Aren't we meant to
be killing them?'

His words didn't console me as we headed into a fairly
rundown estate and I mentally rehearsed the horrors of
not being able to find a vein, or of blowing a vein, or of the
dog, or the owner, or both, getting hysterical.

I could have been forgiven for thinking that there was a
mini street-festival going on as we reached the last house
in the cul-de-sac. An array of old motorbikes and clapped-
out bangers filled the narrow road. I had to park at the far
end and make my way up behind Mikey and Joe as they
carried Bruno through the crowds.

'These are de lads dat 'ad de whip around to do the job,'
explained Joe, seeing my bewildered face. 'Dey all wanted
to be in on it.'

There was just about room for me to squeeze in beside
Bruno as he lay up on the kitchen table, looking slightly
bewildered by his new-found, elevated status within the
community.

I passed over the lead from the electric clippers. Enthusiastic hands somehow managed to pull it to the nearest
socket without strangling anyone.

With Bruno's vein clipped and my syringe loaded, I
stood poised over the aged dog, grateful, at least, that he

seemed to be enjoying life to the end. Mikey whipped a piece of well-worn elastic out of his pocket and handed it to me knowingly as I went to raise the vein. I tied the band around the leg and waited for the vein to pop up at me. I poked at the hardened skin, trying to differentiate the muscles from the vessels and although I could name not only the individual muscles but also their nerve and blood supplies, I couldn't for the life of me find the vein.

An expectant hush fell on my audience as I untied the elastic and clipped a bit more, first right and then left of the initial area. This time, I thought I could finally feel the vein and holding my breath, I poked the needle in the general direction, waiting for the gush of rich blood. Bruno didn't flinch. I peered at the needle, willing some blood to appear, but nothing happened.

'Has 'e got any blood in 'im at all, den?' asked one of the onlookers, breaking the tension as a roar of laughter broke out.

'Well, he's very old, you see, and with his weak heart and that, his veins are collapsed,' I told them, trying to sound like I knew what I was talking about.

I aimed the needle again and this time, not a gush, but a trickle of blood oozed out from the hub of the needle.

Trying to steady my shaking hands, I pushed the needle in fully before attaching the loaded syringe. Slowly, I depressed the plunger, waiting for the head to drop and the wagging tail to quieten. A second later, a bubble appeared at what should have been the vein and Bruno looked over as though to see what I was at. The vein had blown.

With an impending sense of doom, I withdrew my needle.

'Is tha' it, den? Is tha' 'im done?'

I looked down at the syringe and saw that only two millilitres had gone out of the 20-millilitre syringe. Bruno looked as bright as ever.

'Eh, no, I don't think that will do. His vein is so weak – we'll have to try the other one.'

Despite the situation, I could only be grateful that Bruno seemed to be enjoying the whole event and that the owners were far from distraught. Carefully, I clipped the vein on the opposite leg, trying not to think about what I would do if this one blew as well.

The silence fell again as, for the third time, I inserted the needle, this time poking blindly at anything that could possibly resemble a vein. A panic started to rise in me before I heard a voice behind me.

'D'ye wan' me te have a go, luv? I'm good at these.'

A murmer of assent rippled through the room.

'Yeah, good on ye, Paddy!'

'Give yer wan a break.'

Coming over from behind, Paddy took the needle from me as I stepped back in a daze, wondering about the implications of allowing a client to inject a 'Veterinary Surgeon Only' medication.

With practised skill, he adjusted the elastic tie, had a quick feel of the area, spat on his fingers and rubbed them vigorously over the clipped site. He met with a cheer as he inserted the needle, drew a gush of blood and unhesitatingly injected the remainder of the fluid into the old dog who, with a last sigh, made his way out of the world.

'Jaysus, Paddy, ye should o' been de vet!'

'He'll show ye how to do it, Doc.'

Hoping forlornly that the deep red flush that was rising up my neck was not too noticeable, I packed up my gear, thankful that in all the excitement I seemed to have been forgotten. Paddy followed me out to the car. He seemed sympathetic as he pushed the wad of crumpled notes into my hand.

'Don't worry,' he assured me, 'we all have days we can't get the bleedin' vein but, sure, if ye ever need a hand, ye know where to find me!'

CHAPTER SEVEN

LEARNING
ON THE JOB

The weeks seemed to fly by and I became totally caught up with the clients and their cases. Justin tended to leave me to it, partially, he claimed, because, being only two years out of college himself, he didn't have all that much experience either. To me, however, he seemed to be so terribly competent, compared to myself. The great burst of enthusiasm with which I had started was gradually being eroded by the ups and downs of veterinary practice which, in time, I would come to accept as part of the nature of the job.

Before we qualified, one of our lecturers had warned us that within six months in practice we would have lost some of our initial confidence. She was wrong. It took a mere six weeks before the first bitch I spayed had herniated, a horse castration had bled and I had sent a gelding with a foot abscess into the veterinary college for stifle

X-rays – the foot abscess burst in the horse-box on the way in and along with it, my brimming confidence.

Because of Michael's incapacity, I had begun working before many of my classmates, most of whom had wisely decided to take a well-earned break before surrendering themselves to the whims of the general public.

A few sympathetic friends listened as I recounted my tales of woe. My mobile phone bill for those six weeks was more than all my other expenditures put together. I think the friends were secretly horrified by my appalling blunders.

'But I thought you had castrated horses before?'

'I had!' I wailed. 'And they were fine – I just don't know what happened to this one.'

'But you got an honour in surgery, Gill! You'd done loads of suturing before,' consoled another friend.

'Yeah, but five days later they brought the bitch back. The lump was the size of a melon. The first thing the owners wanted to know was if they could sue me for it.'

'How could I have missed a foot abscess?' I asked Justin, who seemed to be amused by my bewilderment.

'Ah well, sure, you'll know better next time.'

That didn't make this time any better.

And night time was no better. My nights became filled with bizarre dreams in which I relived the day's cases. One week, we had a litter of pups with a particularly virulent form of the canine parvo virus. We lost quite a few of them and it was really getting to me. I knew it had to stop when I woke up in a sweat one night to ask Donal if he had had his parvo vaccinations yet!

Luckily, just before I started filling in application forms for a job in McDonald's, a few of my friends finally did start to work. I wished them well as sincerely as I could, but, secretly, I was dreading to hear how great they all would be!

And then the tales of woe started to pour in. It was hard to believe, but my cock-ups weren't as bad as some. Suddenly, I began to feel there was hope.

So gradually that I didn't really notice it happening, things started to improve. Animals stopped dying. Occasionally, I even cured one! Once in a while, I surprised myself by knowing what was actually wrong with one before handing out a variety of coloured pills.

I couldn't believe it when one day I clearly heard a farmer in the reception room asking for 'the young lady vet, please'.

Once, as I explained the options to the anxious owner of a very old and arthritic dog, she took my hand in hers and assured me that she would do whatever I thought was best. She had absolute faith in me. Unfortunately, the dog died, but I don't think I was directly responsible for it.

I knew things were definitely looking up when the nightmares stared to lessen. Getting a half-way decent night's sleep was a big improvement.

'Don't worry,' I confidently reassured my friends. 'It does get better!'

'Well, it couldn't possibly get worse,' replied one, as he filled me in on his latest disaster.

Needless to say, though, despite everything you learned in college and despite all the experience in the world, there are some cases that you could never be prepared for.

* * *

One morning, I had to attend an urgent call in a housing estate in one of Dublin's dodgier inner-city suburbs. For once, I knew where I was going, as I had attended the family before to scan one of their trotting horses to see if she was in foal. They were a tough bunch, but very genuine.

Despite this, I still felt some trepidation as I neared my destination. This time, the call was to attend the guard dog. I had admired him from a distance on my previous visit although his enormous, arched frame and snarling teeth didn't invite any further inspection. He could be best described as a cross between a Rhodesian Ridgeback and a Rottweiler, with a bit of German Shepherd thrown in for good measure. Rambo meant business. The Murphys proudly informed me that theirs was the only house in the estate that hadn't been broken into in the last year. I wasn't surprised.

Armed with my strongest muzzle and a fast-acting sedative, I knocked on the door of number twenty-nine. One of the sons, Deco, yanked the door open while I was still holding on to the knocker. Although he was only a child, he looked wise beyond his years; streetwise anyway.

'Missus, come in quick. Rambo's bollixed!'

'What happened him?'

He led me out to the shed in the tiny yard, talking as he went. 'There wasn't a thing wrong with 'im an hour ago. There was a bit of a scrap on de Avenue and de pigs arrived. Some lad tried to jump over de wall to get away an' Rambo let out a bit of a woof. Yer man fucked off. But when I came back out afterwards, Rambo was knackered – eyes rollin' in 'is 'ead and shakin' all over de place.'

Instantly, my mind was going over the different forms of epilepsy – sudden onset, variable recovery – but still, I would have expected the dog to have improved by now. When I saw the giant beast lying in his kennel, however, my diagnosis changed. Without ever having seen such a case before, it was all too obvious. Rambo was stoned.

The usually tense muscles were slumped in total indo-lence and his tail lazily thumped out a friendly rhythm. He gazed at me blearily through glazed eyes, as though slightly surprised to see me. I couldn't help laughing as I knelt down to examine him, thinking of our ethics lectures in col-lege, where the morals of tail docking, or the rights and wrongs of breeding brood bitches, had been the usual topics of discussion. Or maybe I had missed the lecture on how to deal with a stoned guard-dog, in the sole charge of an under-age child. I sobered up a bit as I realised that I must also have missed the lecture on the treatment of the same patient. I hadn't a clue. In all probability, Deco and his friends were more likely to know what to do than I was.

'Deco, he's been doped and it's very important that I know what exactly he's had, so that I can treat him prop-erly.'

'What d'ye mean he's doped? I swear to Jaysus I'm clean. I never touch the bleedin' stuff. Me Ma'd kill me.'

Looking into his troubled face, I was inclined to believe him. He had no reason to lie to me. Drug-dealing was commonplace in this particular estate but only the guards would be seen as a threat. A thought occurred to me …

'You said he was okay when the guards arrived out on the Avenue and when someone tried to climb the wall, didn't you?'

'Yeah, there wasn't a bother on 'im. He let a woof out of 'im and nearly caught yer man by the bollix when 'e tried to hop over. Ye could hear 'im roaring all the way down the street.'

I tried to suppress the laughter that was threatening to erupt. 'Is there any way the man could have dumped anything into the yard when he tried to climb over?'

'Jaysus, Doc, you're probably right. I know yer man and 'is brudder's been done before for dealing.'

A quick search around the yard revealed two torn plastic bags. Traces of a fine, white powdery substance adhered to the plastic with big drools of saliva.

Once again, I was hindered by my ignorance. Normally, the staff at the Beaumont Poison Centre provide excellent information on the treatment of any form of poisoning. I think it amuses them to deal with a veterinary surgeon instead of a doctor. But you have to know what substance you're dealing with. I could imagine their reaction if I rang wondering what to do with a very chilled-out looking dog, surrounded by a quantity of empty plastic bags.

'Do you know what he deals in, Deco?'

'I haven't a bleedin' clue. He's a bad fucker 'e is. I'd 'ave nothing to do with him.'

I wasn't brave enough or foolish enough to try to find out myself. In the greater scheme of things, my life was worth more to me than Rambo's.

As so often happens in veterinary, I resorted to what is officially termed as 'symptomatic therapy' which, roughly translated, means you don't know what else to do. The only vaguely useful thing that I did was to administer an emetic to force Rambo to vomit what was left of the substance in his stomach.

By the time I had left, Rambo was snoring peacefully. I hoped he would be okay. Occasionally he would yelp and his legs would paddle frantically as though he were hallucinating.

'Let me know how he gets on, anyway,' I called out to Deco as I drove off.

I didn't hear any more for a couple of weeks until one evening when Deco's brother arrived at the surgery looking for some worm doses for the horse. Apparently Rambo had slept for most of the day and then had made an uneventful recovery.

Sometimes the best learning is done on the job.

CHAPTER EIGHT

A HELPING HAND

I groaned inwardly when I saw my clients in the waiting-room. Two girls – probably sisters by the look of them – clutching a small box, containing God only knew what. Both were dressed in identical shiny track-suits and brand-name runners. They had the hardened look of kids that hadn't had it easy growing up.

I didn't like the idea of treating any animal with only children present but I knew I would be wasting my time asking these girls to come back with their parents. The only way I would see them was if something went wrong and then, not only would I meet the parents, but also a variety of brothers or cousins or neighbours, who would join in the fight. Equally, I knew that whatever was in the cardboard box was probably all that those girls had.

Reluctantly, I sighed and waved them in. At least, I thought, the parents would hardly be the litigious type – much more likely to slash my tyres or something. The taller of the two plonked the box on the consulting table.

'His name's Geronimo,' she muttered, staring sullenly at the floor. Mistaking my hesitation, she proceeded to pull a plastic bag out of her back pocket, containing an assortment of loose change, probably about five euro or so.

'I have money.'

I carefully put my hand in through a crack in the top of the box and groped around until I felt a furry creature wriggling about inside. Something felt wrong. I firmly grabbed hold of the little animal but my heart sank when I saw what emerged. Why did it have to be this one? There, in the palm of my hand, lay a large tumour and attached to it was the emaciated remains of a gerbil. I pitied the tiny creature as he squirmed helplessly in my hands. Clearly, there was only one solution for him but I wasn't quite sure how the stony-faced girls would take it.

Gently, I explained in terms that they would understand, that Geronimo would not be going home with them. A deathly silence followed, until I noticed a small tear trickling down the grubby face of the younger girl. As I turned to get her a tissue, the older girl also noticed.

'Will ye stop yer whingin', Sharon!' and then the silence was shattered as the two of them began to sob hysterically, in long loud gulps, as though the world would end.

The usual platitudes that 'He's had a good life' and that, 'He won't suffer any more' were lost in the din that they made.

In desperation, I pushed the bag of money that was still sitting on the table back towards them.

'Why don't you buy another gerbil on the way home?'

As suddenly as it had started, the mass hysteria stopped.

Beams of delight radiated from the two tear-stained faces and, as though they were afraid that I would change my mind, they grabbed the bag and ran out the door without a further glance at the unfortunate Geronimo. Once they had gone, I put a fiver of my own in the till, and drew up one millilitre of the lethal injection into a tiny syringe. The little body went limp in my hand before I had finished injecting him.

In the usual bedlam of a Monday afternoon, I had soon forgotten all about my two young clients. The first patient of the evening was a dainty-looking poodle, who trotted in happily on the end of her owner's lead. Suddenly, as I was lifting her up on to the table, I heard a racket breaking out in the waiting-room. As the commotion grew louder, I tried to smile reassuringly at my client, but then the door burst open and a large, untidy woman entered, followed by Liz, looking even more harassed than usual. A battered cage containing about half a dozen young, fluffy gerbils was thrown on to the table with a violence that caused the alarmed poodle to let out a shrill yelp before jumping into the arms of its owner, who promptly disappeared at speed out the door.

'Ye stupid cow, ye! I never wanted that bleedin' rat in me house in the first place and now them two bitches of mine come home with six more. If yez ever give dem money again, my Paddy will come down and thump ye one!' With that she stalked out, slamming the door behind her.

Liz and I looked at each other in bewilderment before breaking into helpless fits of laughter.

I got a few funny looks from the remaining clients in the waiting room and finished off the clinic under the watchful, beady eyes of six gerbils.

Much to the disgust of Popeye, the resident cat, they remained with us until, one by one, we found homes for them – apart from the smallest little fawn one, who eventually gained resident status and was christened Olive.

CHAPTER NINE

PRACTISE WHAT
YOU PREACH

I was a bit taken aback by the man's request. When he had come into the surgery for a 'quick word', I had assumed that it was about something four-legged. However, he introduced himself as the principal of the neighbouring girls' secondary school, and explained that they had organised a special day in aid of World Animal Week. As part of the event, they usually had the local vet in to give a talk, but, as I was a 'lady vet', as he so politely put it, he thought that his students would be more interested in hearing about the career from my point of view. I hesitantly inquired as to the nature of the talk and roughly how many were expected to attend.

'Only a handful of transition-year students,' he replied. 'Ten or fifteen minutes at most – just explaining to them about the sort of work you do and how you got started. I know you're new to the job but that's all the better from their point of view. There are some really great kids in the school but between me and you, most of them don't get much support from home. It would be great to give them a bit of incentive.'

I felt it would be churlish of me to refuse.

'I'm really not used to public speaking,' I replied hesitantly, 'but I'll give it a go if you're sure it's only for a few of them.'

'You don't know how much I appreciate it. I know the girls will just love you.' He shook my hand warmly before leaving me with final instructions about the schedule and how to get to the school.

The next morning I tried to fob it off on Justin, but he was having none of it.

'Not a chance!' he laughed. 'And, anyway, didn't he want a female vet? Waste of time me going out.'

Liz assured me it would be 'great fun'. 'And anyway,' she continued, 'it'll get you out of doing that fat bitch spay that's booked in for Friday morning.'

Every night that week, I planned to prepare my speech, but one day followed another at the usual hectic pace and it was the morning of the talk before I finally found myself putting pen to paper. I briefly described the necessary qualities I thought it took to become a decent vet – such laudable characteristics as having a deep concern for animal welfare, the ability to communicate in a kind and caring way with their owners, the stamina to work odd hours at irregular intervals, and all the rest of it.

A vividly coloured banner hung over the school gates, welcoming all visitors to World Animal Week.

There was a buzz of excitement in the air as throngs of schoolgirls milled around the yard, enjoying the freedom of a non-uniform day in honour of the occasion. I secretly hoped that my handful of transition years would be a little more restrained than this lot.

Mr Walsh, the principal, met me as arranged in the staff room. He looked suspiciously guilty as he announced in a casual tone that there had been a slight change of plan. I got the distinct feeling that I was being set up.

'The girls decided that we should charge a euro per head and open the talk to the whole school. I told them you wouldn't mind. You don't, do you?'

I did actually – a lot. But what could I say at this stage with only ten minutes to go? 'Exactly how many do you think there'll be?'

'Oh, only about five hundred or so,' he replied airily, as though it were only a slight addition to the original number. 'But don't worry, I know they're going to love you. They're all wound up to ninety, they're so excited.'

That was exactly what I had feared.

'There's only one other thing. To make a bit of a day of it, I've invited over six lads and a few supporters from the local boys' school for a debate on cruelty to animals afterwards. To make it worthwhile, we've extended your speech to roughly an hour or so.'

'But my speech is only fifteen minutes,' I blustered, 'and it's for fifteen-year-old girls, not eleven to eighteen-year-old girls and boys.'

'Don't you be worrying about prepared speeches,' he reassured me soothingly. 'Improvisation always works best. Trust me, I'm a drama teacher.'

Without giving me a chance to object, he marshalled me down a corridor and led me into a hall that to me looked roughly the size of The Point Depot. It was packed with masses of excitable teenagers. A herd of angry bullocks couldn't have competed with the ear-splitting racket they were creating. He then ushered me up on to the platform. As I stood there surveying the crowd, I noticed that nobody seemed to be remotely interested in my presence. In fact, no one even seemed to have noticed that I was there at all. At that moment, I understood roughly how the Christians must have felt before being thrown to the lions. I was terrified, and would have given anything to be somewhere else.

As I glanced frantically around the crowded hall, I noticed Mr Walsh discreetly tucked in a corner, waving towards the microphone and beckoning me to begin. I stepped cautiously towards it, tapped on it once or twice and spoke in what I hoped was a clear and confident voice.

'Now if you could all take your seats, please,' I began bravely, 'I'd like to introduce myself.'

No one paid me the slightest bit of attention.

With an increasing sense of desperation, I tapped the mike again and repeated myself in a louder voice. One or two students briefly interrupted their animated conversation and threw a quick glance in my direction. I smiled hopefully at them – but in vain. They looked away again and resumed where they had left off. A cold sweat was starting to break out on my forehead when one of the older girls, seeming to notice my distress, leapt up on to the stage, grabbed the mike from me and roared into it: 'For Jaysus' sake, lads, this is the bleedin' vet! Will yez ever give 'er a chance?'

I stared in horror at Mr Walsh, expecting double detentions all around; instead, he smiled encouragingly at the girl, rewarding her initiative. He hadn't been joking when he told me earlier that he encouraged 'his girls' to work things out for themselves. He felt that it was character-building.

At that moment, my character felt like disappearing into the proverbial hole in the ground. However, the expectant silence that had suddenly been created left me with no option but to falteringly begin my prepared speech – the fifteen-minute speech that somehow I was now supposed to make last an entire hour.

I've heard of padding before, but developing fifteen minutes into sixty was a tall order. I was acutely aware of my audience's attention drifting in and out of my grasp as I discussed the role of a vet and the basic concepts of animal welfare. Occasionally, I noticed the sympathetic glances from the haggard-looking teachers dotted around the hall. I kept my eye on the clock on the far end of the wall and was fully convinced that it was stopped for about twenty minutes or so. I flirted briefly with the idea of opening the talk up to a 'questions and answers' session to fill up the time but dismissed it just as quickly. I could well imagine the sort of questions I would be asked.

I felt like a cat with nine lives, eight of which I passed through in rapid succession over the fifty minutes. At that stage, I decided enough was enough, and brought the talk to a close by wishing the students luck with their fund-raising campaign and thanking them for their attention.

A rapturous round of applause broke out, probably with relief that I had finally finished and they could now get on to the serious business of getting a better look at the local talent in the shape of the visiting debating team and supporters from the boys' school.

As I left the hall, I was intercepted by a kindly group of teachers.

'Well done. They're a bit of a lively bunch, aren't they?'

Understatement of the year.

'Do you know,' confided one of the younger, more energetic ones, 'I think you're marvellous to do the job you do. I wouldn't swap with you for all the money in the world.'

The feeling was mutual.

As I drove out of the school grounds, I felt as though I had worked through a full week on my own, night and day, single-handedly. I couldn't face going back to work just yet and, knowing it wasn't a busy day, I switched off the phone and pulled into the local pub for dinner and a pot of strong tea.

* * *

Half an hour later I was beginning to feel that I might just about have survived the ordeal. Reluctantly, I rang the surgery to see if there were any calls still waiting to be done.

'There's three cattle to be skulled up in Joe Lynch's

place,' Liz told me. 'Justin is still operating on the Westie from last night but he said if you want, he'll go out and do the cattle with you afterwards.'

Skulling was usually carried out in the autumn and involved removing the horns from cattle in order to prevent them from injuring each other or their handlers. In older cattle it was done using either a large guillotine-type chopper known (at least in these parts) as a crange, or by sawing them off with a piece of embryotomy wire. Preferably it was done while the cattle were still calves, at which stage the soft bud-like horns could be simply burned off (a process known as debudding), but in areas like the one I was currently working in, dominated by part-time farmers, they tended not to think about such things until the calves were too old. By that stage the hard, thick, horny material made it much more difficult to do.

'Tell Justin thanks very much, anyway, but I'll go on up and have a go at them. If I get stuck, I can always give him a shout.'

I was glad to see the farmer standing waiting for me with the three cattle ready in the crush as I drove up the rough driveway to a field behind a council housing estate.

'How are you?' I called out as I pulled on the rough wet gear over my boots. Skulling was notoriously messy work.

'Not too bad. And yourself?'

'Ah sure, things could be worse. I see you have the cattle ready for me, anyway. They're a bit on the big side, aren't they?'

'Yeah, I'm sorry about that. I meant to do them as calves but what with my mother not being well and everything, they got a bit strong on me.' Joe's mother had died during the summer after a long battle with cancer. He and his wife had cared for her to the bitter end, despite having an ever-increasing brood of their own to look after. I felt that under the circumstances a lecture on the disadvantages of skulling at such an advanced age would be out of place.

'Not to worry, we'll soon sort them out,' I replied, suddenly wishing I had taken Justin up on his offer.

The crush was a home-made one, but looked to be strong enough for the job. In my four months' experience of testing cattle to date, it wasn't unusual for me to spend a large part of my day chasing breakaway rebel cattle across fields as they dragged in their wake the shattered segments of the crush that had once contained them. The part-time farmers whom we dealt with on the outskirts of the city tended not to be as well-equipped as the farmers in the more agricultural areas. My main worry with Joe's crush was that it had no front gate in which to lock the heads. For someone as inexperienced as I was, you needed the cattle's heads to be held securely while the procedure was being carried out, and Joe wouldn't have been the best of stockmen.

After a few false starts, I dropped a rope halter over the head of the first one and rapidly tied it as short as possible before clipping the nose tongs on to his fleshy nostrils. The tongs were reputedly designed to press on specific pressure receptors, causing the release of natural endorphins which supposedly helped to calm the animal. Unfortunately, this did not have the desired effect on my patient. His mouth opened wide and he bellowed with an indignant roar. His comrades eagerly took up the cause and joined in.

'Just hang on to the tongs for me while I inject him, will you, please, Joe?'

I inserted the needle just under the bony ridge between the eye and the horn to inject the local anaesthetic, thus ensuring that the process of removing the horn would be painless for the animal. The bullock's distress was entirely due to the unfamiliarity of being handled and restrained. I repeated the process on the other side before releasing him. Joe warned me about the next bullock – a small, black wiry Limousin.

'Watch yourself with that one – he's a bit of a bugger!'

He looked it, too, as he snorted at me while I poised over him, ready to drop the halter over his head. As it fell, he whipped it out of my hands with a menacing shake of his horns. It took three attempts before I managed to catch him and he roared incessantly while I injected him. When I finished the last bullock, I sat back to wait the few minutes before the first one would be ready. It's nearly easier to do a large number of cattle because by the time you have them all injected, the first one is ready to be dehorned. However, after the traumatic experiences of that morning, I didn't mind stopping as the minutes passed by with idle chat between myself and Joe.

All too soon, it was time to start the actual process of dehorning. As I warily eyed the thick horns, I wondered how I would acquit myself. The first bullock was most displeased to find himself ensnared in the halter for the second time and roared balefully, encouraging his comrades to join in the battle. Most vets have a personal preference for either the crange or the wire, but, as I had never tried either of them before, it was a toss of a coin as to which one I would go for. I decided on the crange.

With Joe holding the mighty head, I angled the blades at what I thought was the correct angle and tried to close over the mighty arms of the vicious-looking weapon. Just as I was about to give up and try the wire, the blades met with an almighty crack and the giant horn shot off into the distance.

As I stopped to catch my breath, I noticed a slight problem: the side of the crush, until now brilliantly white, was now covered with fountains of bright red blood, cascading down the roughened surface. What I had thought was the correct angle of the blade obviously wasn't. Jets of blood spurted out of the bony horn base. I wasn't terribly concerned by the amount of blood – it's amazing how a little blood can look like an awful lot – but I was wondering how on earth I would stop it. It was usual to have one or two bleeders from the small vessels supplying the horns when skulling and it didn't take long to grab hold of the vessel and twist the elasticated walls until the bleeding stooped, but in this case I didn't know where to begin. Joe's only comment as he watched the vivid display was: 'By God, that's as good as any fireworks show!' Luckily, the bullock appeared to be totally unaware of my consternation. If anything, he seemed to be slightly amused by the bright red patterns on the wall. The other two snorted suspiciously but weren't enormously put out. I became so engrossed in the fiddly job of pulling the vessels that I didn't notice the occasional spurt of hot blood that hit my face. When the job was done to my satisfaction, I wiped away the irritating drips that had begun to gather on the tip of my nose and puffed liberal amounts of antibiotic powder onto the freshly-cut horn base. The bullock seemed none the worse for wear.

The second horn wasn't quite so bad as I slightly altered the angle of the blades but the bullock was, by now, getting bored and shook his head impatiently while I tried to seal the bleeding vessels.

Number two proved much more difficult to catch a second time and soon my knuckles were cut and bleeding as he carelessly thrashed me against the rough wall. I finally managed to secure him to the strongest post.

'I think I'll try the wire on this lad,' I said casually to Joe. 'He mightn't bleed so much. The heat created by the wire tends to seal the vessels.'

'Well, sure, it's up to yourself. You're the expert!'

If only he knew.

'Get a good hold on the tongs there, Joe,' I told him. 'I've a feeling this one won't be quite so tolerant.'

'Don't worry. I have him good and tight. He won't be able to budge a muscle,' he replied with a confidence that I didn't share as two wicked eyes glared at me contemptuously from beneath a mass of wiry hair.

I didn't have a proper handle to tie the wire on to and, in my innocence, I wrapped each end around the jaws of a forceps, thinking that would do the job. Carefully, I positioned the wire around the base of the horn and started to draw it back and forward in even, measured strokes. The strong wire, designed to cut through bone, bit into my tender flesh before it started to make any impression on the horn itself. Despite my misgivings, the bullock stood as though immobilised. I was afraid to stop to reposition the wire away from my raw fingers in case he would change his mind. I sawed desperately, back and forth, as the wire ate into the flinty horn. With a sense of relief, I watched the smoke start to billow up from the surface, knowing that at least this one wouldn't bleed so much. This was definitely a better plan. I was beginning to gasp by the time I had got half way through the horn but I kept on going, ignoring the burning pains in my torn fingers. I fell backwards as the last section broke off and the horn fell harmlessly to the ground.

'By God, you wouldn't want to do that job too often!' said Joe, eyeing me speculatively as the sweat poured down my sticky face. I didn't bother to reply, but just grinned back at him as I tried to catch my breath.

The bullock was still standing quietly, much to my amazement, so, making the most of the temporary truce, I started on the next horn. I was getting well into it when I suddenly found myself sprawled on the ground, still grimly holding on to the forceps.

'What the hell happened there?' I asked Joe, as I watched the bullock plunge and thrash in the rickety crush. Suddenly, I wasn't so sure it would hold this furious beast.

'The bugger! He just lost his wick. I hadn't a chance of holding him. He whipped the tongs clean out of my hands.'

Joe looked around him in bewilderment, wondering what had become of the tongs. Then I spied a piece of gleaming metal about twenty yards away. It was half of the handle, snapped right through the metal by the sheer force as it hit the wall. We never found the rest.

'Well, we'll just have to do without it so,' I replied, sounding a lot more cheerful than I felt.

Now that the bullock had scored a point, he was determined to finish the battle. I quickly wrapped the wire back around the remaining horn and sawed as fast as I could but it wasn't so easy this time with his powerful head thrashing in all directions. The other two on either side, who had seemed relatively docile up to now, were inspired by his temper and did their level best to out-bawl him. For one sickening moment, I heard a sharp crack as one of the upright planks in the crush gave way under the assault. I kept going. If the crush broke now, there would be a one-horned bullock roaming the Dublin mountains for some time to come.

It was at this stage, with the battle in full cry, that I noticed a young girl making her way up the drive. She stopped some distance off, obviously horrified by the blood-stained walls, the roars of the cattle and my sweating body being lashed around on one end of a long horn.

I didn't stop to explain until the horn dropped to the ground and I staggered away from my roaring adversary.

'Hi, you must be Joe's daughter?' I panted. 'This isn't as bad as it looks. He's just a mad bullock that resents human handling,' I added reassuringly.

'Claire loves to help with the cattle, don't you, love?' said

Joe proudly. 'This is all my fault, Claire. If I had done them as calves, it wouldn't have been half so bad.'

I flashed a grateful look of thanks at him. It would have helped too if I had been a bit more experienced at the job!

Claire was staring at me with a puzzled look on her face. 'I know you from somewhere, don't I?' Before I could deny it, it came to her with a sense of total shock and outrage. 'You're the vet who gave the talk on animal welfare this morning, aren't you?'

I just couldn't believe my luck.

'You'd think you'd practise what you preach!' she admonished me, with a look of scorn that only a teenager could muster.

My explanations about the local anaesthetic and how hill cattle roar with the upset of being handled were wasted as she glared disbelievingly at me. In fairness to Joe, he tried to back me up but, naturally, Claire knew more than her father.

Oh well, I thought, it really was one of those days. I sighed at my shattered reputation as I went on to do the last bullock. The procedure went a little more smoothly than the last two but Claire was clearly not at all impressed.

Once out of the crush, the cattle grazed contentedly as though the whole ordeal had been forgotten. I looked wistfully at the bleeding welts on my hands and I knew there was no point in explaining that I was probably in more pain than they were. Nobody cares about vet welfare!

I washed the instruments off before bringing them back to the car. Slug was delighted by the smell of fresh hot blood and did her best to lick it off from anywhere she could reach. It was on days like these that she really loved her job.

As I packed away the gear, Claire gleefully dropped the final bombshell. 'Do you know you used the F-word twice during your talk?'

I had a habit of cursing during moments of stress. In fact, with hindsight, I was surprised I had only used it twice. I thanked God that my rising colour would be hidden by the blood stains on my face. I pitied Joe and his wife living with a little horror like that.

'I think you could do with a cup of tea and a wash,' Joe said, grinning sympathetically at me.

In fairness to Paula, Joe's wife, she did her best to contain her shock as what must have looked like a blood-spattered extra from a Dracula film appeared at her kitchen door. However, the toddler playing away contentedly on the floor took one look at me before disappearing with a high-pitched wail into the next room.

Throughout my first summer of work, I often had to wash down with the power hose in the yard, but after a particularly dirty job I had become accustomed to being invited into the dairy or even the kitchen. This time was the worst yet. I cringed with embarrassment as Paula enquired kindly, 'Would you like to take a bath while I boil the kettle for a cup of tea?'

CHAPTER TEN

THE CAT-HUNT

Late nights and Sunday afternoons were the usual times for calls from the various animal sanctuaries. All vets do a certain amount of animal welfare work but the times when the general public suddenly chose to take an interest in such issues always amused me. It was amazing how, on the way into the pub, people would happily walk past an innocent night-time rambler but, after closing time, they would feel morally obliged to rescue him and save him from his fate. In their well lubricated sense of conscientiousness, somebody would always feel the need to ensure prompt veterinary attention for the animal who, in reality, was probably not lost at all. Of course, when it came to footing the bill, these kind-hearted souls would magically disappear, satisfied that they had adequately fulfilled their obligation to society.

Equally, on Sunday afternoons, especially on rainy ones, it was not uncommon to get a call from one of the sanctuaries with a request to attend a call from a member of the public – presumably someone for whom getting a vet out would break the monotony of an otherwise dull day.

This Sunday was to be no different. I had just returned home from treating a pedigree calf with a broken leg when the phone rang.

'Hi, Gillian. Sorry to bother you but I've just had a frantic call from an estate on the northside. They say there's a cat after getting badly mauled by a collie in one of the gardens.'

Rita was a full-time employee at one of the local sanctuaries and we had been involved in a few hairy cases together. She was well used to these Sunday-afternoon call-outs and had often sympathised with me when, having driven twenty or so miles to an 'urgent' case, I would arrive to find the weather had cleared up and the person who had reported the case had headed off to the beach – the animal forgotten under the changed circumstances.

'It's no problem, Rita. Do you have an owner?'

'I'm afraid not. Apparently it's been straying in the area for quite a while and it's fairly wild. Of course nobody bothered about it before now. I would imagine it's a case for euthanasia.'

In many of these cases euthanasia was the unfortunate but also the only realistic option for the animal. Where literally dozens of healthy cats and kittens are put to sleep every week, it is hopeless to try re-homing the really wild ones that take weeks or even months to tame. The best we can offer in a situation where an animal can't fend for itself is a dignified and painless death.

I scribbled down the address and grabbed a cat-cage

before making my way back down the road in the direction of Buttercup Valley. I often wondered which inspired planner had chosen the names for some of Dublin's less salubrious housing estates. Titles such as Primrose Lawns or Heatherview Gardens seemed incongruous in the miniature concrete jungles where not so much as a blade of grass was visible. I could never decide if it was a subconscious effort to make up for the lack of green spaces or just a slightly dubious attempt at black humour.

I had a rough idea where Buttercup Valley was to be found along with an assortment of Buttercup Lawns, Rises, Views, Drives, Groves and many others. I could never figure out if these estates had had any signposts in the first place and if they had all been removed by vandals. I knew from past experience that stopping to ask for directions in such places was a bad idea as you were likely to get mobbed by a group of kids or, at the very worst, have a few weapons hurled through your windscreen.

I kept my eyes down and drove at speed past the gangs of curious kids gathered on each corner, swerving to avoid the burnt-out car in the middle of the road and narrowly avoiding a collision with a piebald galloping down the street, spurred on by his two juvenile riders.

Eventually, having driven up and down most of the minor roadways, I came across an excited group of youngsters congregated in the tiny front garden of a rundown house. As they saw the car approaching, they jumped out in front of me to wave me down. I decided this must be the right place. Battling through the crowd of excited onlookers, I made my way around to the boot to get the cat-cage.

'Missus, can I hold yer bag for ye?'

'Auld Rover had a bleedin' great time. He hasn't run as fast in years!'

'Ye'll have some job catching Tiger – 'e's a mad bastard.'

Oh great, I thought, they hadn't even caught the cat. I had the distinct feeling that this whole journey was going to be yet another waste of time.

I tried to adopt an orderly approach to what seemed like an increasingly chaotic situation.

'I don't have a bag, thanks, but you can bring in the cage if you like.' I made a habit of not carrying any drugs on these calls. In the past I had learned, much to my amazement, of the street value of some of our sedatives, anaesthetic agents and other medicines. I once heard of a friend whose car was robbed of a large quantity of small white worm tablets. The perpetrator was found selling them for twenty euro apiece in town that night!

Rover, I assumed, was the elderly, tired but contented-looking collie-type dog flopped out on the grass. So he was the culprit. Clearly, the exertion of a live chase had brought him to the point of exhaustion.

The kids became increasingly noisy as I approached the front door and when their clamour reached loudspeaker level, I took a deep breath and roared at the top of my voice: 'WILL YOU ALL BE QUIET, PLEASE!'

For about two seconds there was relative peace and then it started again as they outdid each other yelling.

'Yeah, did yez hear what she said? Just shut the fuck up!'

'Chris, if ye don't shut yer bleedin' trap, I'll box ye.'

'Would yez just let yer wan talk?'

'QUIET!' I bellowed again, as two of the lads started a free-for-all brawl in the background. The ferocity of my voice obviously had some effect as a subdued silence fell on the onlookers. Seizing my opportunity, I marched up to the dazed-looking woman in the doorway, who was dragging on what I first presumed to be a cigarette but which closer inspection revealed to be a joint of some kind. She glared at me suspiciously as though I posed a threat to her hash-induced state of tranquillity.

'You must be Mrs Mullan,' I began hesitantly. 'I believe you have an injured cat.'

I never found out if indeed she was Mrs Mullan, as she gazed through me with expressionless eyes. One of the younger kids pushed his way forward through the crowd with a great air of self-importance.

'Don't mind me Ma, Missus. She's spaced oura her trolley. Come on into the back garden. Rover ran de cat into de shed. He's still in it.'

I followed the spiky-haired youngster past Mrs Mullan who eyed me warily without saying a word. I was beginning to wonder if I was forming an hallucination in her fuzzy brain.

She didn't appear to either care or notice as literally dozens of kids trooped past her through the house.

'Here, Spike, we'll give yez a hand catchin' the moggy.'

Whatever about the kids, I shut the door firmly on the disappointed-looking Rover. I think he was ready for round two. Mind you, I thought he was probably the one with the best chance of catching the cat.

Spike brought me up to a battered-looking shed at the

end of the garden and flung open the door. 'He's in dere!' he informed me triumphantly.

I stared in dismay at the tiny shed, packed to the ceiling with various bits and pieces of broken furniture, old bikes and bulging rubbish bins. There was no sign of my patient.

As I became accustomed to the dim light, however, I was able to pick out a pair of furious green eyes watching me from the darkest corner. I could just about make out the outline of a vividly-striped, orange feline crouching behind a broken chair. This was not going to be easy.

'Okay, everyone out!' I ordered, pulling on a pair of long, protective gloves, in what seemed like a vain precaution to prevent my arms from being shredded. I shut the door firmly behind me and gingerly approached the hissing cat.

'Here, puss, puss, puss,' I coaxed encouragingly.

Tiger eyeballed me warningly from his safe haven as I slowly extended my hand towards him. Just as I was about to grab the scruffy coat, he darted past me, bringing with him half a dozen old paint cans. It was at this stage that Spike could obviously contain himself no longer and opened the door. An orange bolt of lightning shot out past him.

A cheer erupted from the crowd gathered outside. Obviously this was high entertainment on a boring Sunday afternoon.

In the confusion that followed, nobody seemed to notice that the cat had made his way off to the far corner of the garden and perched himself on top of the boundary wall. As far as you could see, rows of similar breezeblock walls interrupted the narrow strips of garden. A few heads, both human and canine, began appearing over the wall-tops as the cat sat glaring indignantly at the scene. I could see a graze on the end of his tail, obviously inflicted by the gallant Rover, but, judging by the speed with which he had reached safety on top of the wall, I wasn't particularly worried about him. Cats have great healing powers and one that couldn't be caught generally wasn't in too much danger.

I was just about to call a halt to the whole proceedings when a stringy little terrier caught sight of the cat and set up a lusty baying as though his life depended on it. Within seconds, dogs appeared out of nowhere and joined in the bloodcurdling cry. No pack of hunting hounds could have been more enthusiastic.

'Listen, lads,' I roared, 'the cat's okay. Leave him alone until the dogs settle down again. He'll only get hurt if he comes down off the wall.' But it was too late. Before I could stop him, one of the kids had got the bright idea of grabbing a sweeping brush to evict the cat from his safe haven in a vain attempt to catch him. Flailing claws flew in all directions as the cat spat vehemently at his assailant before being knocked off his perch in a clean sweep into the next garden.

A joyous baying rang out anew as the cat, followed by a pack of dogs, followed by a horde of children, followed lastly, and at a good distance behind, by myself, raced from garden to garden over the series of natural hurdles formed by the walls.

I don't know how many gardens we crossed, our

numbers increasing at every one, before the unfortunate Tiger eventually found safety on top of a garden shed. A few of the more athletic dogs made several attempts to join him but couldn't quite manage it. From his new-found sanctuary, he glowered down furiously at his tormentors.

'Now leave the cat alone,' I panted between gasping breaths. Whoever said small-animal practice was easy? 'He'll make his way down when the dogs are gone.'

It took some time to convince the rebel hunters to disperse – the last few hung on for quite a while until it became obvious that the fun really was over. I hastily explained to the owner of the house whose garden we had ended up in why a pack of excited dogs and children had been charging around her garden. She didn't seem remotely put out.

'Ye look shagged, Missus, if ye don't mind me saying. Will ye have a cup o' tea?' she offered kindly.

I was so frazzled by the events of the last half hour that I was tempted to accept her kind offer, but decided against it in favour of a quick get-away. She accompanied me out to the front door and I was at least saved the indignity of having to scramble back over the walls.

'And don't you be worryin' about de cat. I'll look after de poor little bugger,' she assured me as I began the traipse back to my car, which, by now, was quite some distance away.

I sank back into the seat, having returned the empty cat-cage to the boot, just as the phone rang. I swore silently under my breath. I'd had enough for one day.

'Gillian?' Rita's voice rang out on the other end. 'Don't

worry, I've no more calls for you. I just rang to see how you got on with the cat.'

'Rita, you'll never believe what happened!'

* * *

It was unfortunate that that Sunday was to be my last one working in the area as Michael was due back to work the next morning. I found it hard to believe that five months had passed since graduation day and I felt a little bit older but not much wiser than the day I had started.

Donal and I had gone out for a few drinks the night before with Liz, Justin and Michael, and their respective partners.

'We'd be delighted to have you back any time,' laughed Michael. 'That is, if you'd want to come back!'

I had no more calls for the day so I headed back to the surgery for the last time and I packed up the few belongings of mine that had accumulated over the few months. With Slug curled up in the seat beside me, we headed for home, not knowing what adventures lay in store for us next.

LOCUM

CHAPTER ELEVEN

THE CHRISTMAS CAT

Job interviews in veterinary weren't quite like those for any normal job. The usual procedures of advertising the job, with applicants sending CVs, followed up by at least one interview, were often dispensed with. In a profession where only fifty or so graduates qualified in Ireland each year, the veterinary community was intimate and tight-knit. Everyone knew everyone, or at least everyone knew someone who knew everyone. The fact that students spent most of their holidays seeing practice with the same vets, often the ones they would later look for work from, ensured that the formalities were usually ignored.

Most jobs were filled without ever having been advertised, to the extent that if you saw a job in the papers, it was often an indication that there was something distinctly dodgy about it. At least in that situation, you were always able to log on to the graduate gossip-line and find out exactly what the problem was. Vets who got themselves a bad name as an employer ran into serious problems.

Unfortunately, it worked the other way around as well. If you messed up in one job, you might find yourself having trouble finding another placement.

Several practices had a name for being good places to start off. They had had so many new graduates go through them that you were likely to be quickly forgotten. This made an excellent base from which to make all your early mistakes.

A fortnight before Michael was due to return, I met an elderly vet for an interview. This did not take place in his office, but in the local pub. Once we got chatting, we realised that the job wouldn't suit for various reasons, but that was no excuse to miss out on a social occasion. We stayed until closing time.

Shortly afterwards at a wedding, I met a vet to whom I'd been half-thinking of applying for a job. It was the perfect chance to become acquainted. And that we did. By last orders we were in rare old form and having great *craic* discussing God knows what. I'm sure we were talking great sense too. The only problem arose the next morning – I had absolutely no recollection of whether we had discussed a job at all, or if indeed he might have offered me one. If he did, had I accepted? When I met him it was clear that he had even less recollection of what had been said than I had.

I began putting out feelers by ringing around a few friends to see what was on the market. Not a lot. The few vacant jobs were vacant for a reason. I decided to hold on until something a bit more promising came up.

As a trickle of jobs appeared in the *Irish Veterinary*

Journal, I rang around a few practices.

'Send me a CV and I'll get back to you,' said one.

I did and he didn't.

'Come down some evening for a few drinks,' said another.

I rang to arrange it the next week but he'd already taken someone on.

'Sorry, I hope you don't mind,' he said.

I did, but what could I say?

Initially, I wasn't keen on doing locum work as I felt too inexperienced to work on my own, but time was passing by with no sign of a job. Joyce, a friend of mine from school days, rang me one morning to say that she had mentioned to her own vet, Bill, in Drogheda, that I was looking for work. He was planning to go away for Christmas and as yet had no locum booked. Although I didn't want to be away from home at Christmas, I thought it was too good an opportunity to miss as he had a busy cattle practice. Being a butcher, Christmas was a busy time for Donal and I knew that he would be working solidly until late on Christmas Eve anyway. We arranged that he would drive to Joyce's for dinner on Christmas Day and then stay on with me for the remainder of the week in Bill's house.

The first few days were remarkably quiet as most people who rang, once they heard that Bill was away, decided to hold on until he got back. I decided not to take it too personally. By Christmas morning I was feeling nice and relaxed, and confident that I would be able to manage whatever trivial cases might come in. I was looking forward to Donal coming down as we had only managed a few brief phone calls in the preceding days.

It was not the classic picture-postcard Christmas weather, but dull and miserable; not cold enough to feel Christmassy but damp and dark enough to make you want to stay indoors.

By midday, I had gone to Mass in the local church, and I was on my way over to Joyce's house for dinner where I had arranged to meet Donal. Well and all as we got on, Joyce certainly wasn't used to veterinary life and I hoped that I wouldn't get a call while I was with her. In her regular nine-to-five job the idea of setting aside the wine-glasses on Christmas day to go off on a call to attend a sick animal was just not an option.

'We've planned dinner for one o'clock, so it might be ready for two if we're lucky,' she had laughed the week before.

'Perfect!' I replied, adding on a cautionary note, 'if I get called out, I'll let you know and you just go ahead without me.'

'Called out at dinner-time on Christmas day?' she exclaimed incredulously. 'Who'd be mad enough to do that?'

So far so good, I thought, as I took the exit off the roundabout which would bring me to the housing estate where Joyce and her partner, Greg, lived. I was nice and early and I knew they would both be ready and waiting, in festive mood. There had not been so much as a squeak out of the phones since ten o'clock the previous evening, when a highly indignant – and slightly slurred – lady rang to tell me that one of her husband's friends had thought it would be a good joke to let her prize tropical fish join in the festive spirit and had generously lashed in a good helping of Southern Comfort to their aquarium.

'What,' she enquired forlornly, 'should I do?'

Good question, I thought to myself. I tentatively volunteered the suggestion that she should try changing the water gradually and adding a bit of Stress Coat – the multipurpose supplement for aquarium water.

Great, I thought. So much for a busy cattle practice. I consoled myself that, judging from the sound of her, if the fish were all belly-up in the morning, she probably wouldn't remember who had given her the advice anyway. In fact, it was quite possible that she wasn't even a *bona fide* client and had simply picked the practice number at random out of the local business directory, as was all too common at holiday periods.

Bill had advised me of this and left me with a warning to do emergency calls for clients only.

'If we're not good enough for them during the rest of the year, then we're not good enough for them during the holidays,' he added gruffly, obviously having suffered much from these situations before.

It was almost half-past twelve when I pulled into the corner house, with its coloured fairy lights festooned over the porch and the welcoming glow of lamps in the windows. As yet, there was no sign of Donal's car in the driveway but I knew he wasn't far away.

As I raised my hand to the doorbell, the mobile rang. Surely, I thought, just a well-wisher replying to one of the many early text messages that I had sent that morning.

The breathless woman's voice at the other end soon told me otherwise.

'Is that the vet's?' she enquired hurriedly. 'Thank God!' she exclaimed when I explained that Bill was on holidays but that I was covering for him. 'I knew Mr Ryan had gone away but I didn't know if there would be anyone there in his place.'

'What can I do for you?' I asked patiently.

'Well, I've just come out of a friend's house and as I pulled out, I thought I saw something dart out in front of me. I felt the bump. I got out and couldn't see a thing, but just as I was about to go again, I caught a glimpse of something in the bushes. It's a little cat and I must have run over it.

'Oh, I feel so awful!' she went on. 'I couldn't avoid it, really I couldn't.'

'These things can happen in an instant,' I consoled her. 'The cat may even have been up under your car looking for heat. You had no way of knowing. Does she seem to be badly hurt?' I questioned, all too keenly aware of the delicious cooking smells wafting out from the front porch.

'Oh yes, she's in a terrible state,' the lady continued, her voice quavering. 'She's just lying there and there's blood coming out of her nose. She doesn't seem to be moving at all but I'm afraid to touch her.'

'Do you think she's still alive?' I enquired delicately, not wanting to further upset the obviously distraught woman.

'Oh yes, she is, I can see her little chest moving, all right. Please, can you come out? I know it's Christmas day and you're probably just about to start your dinner,' she said as though reading my thoughts, 'but I feel so awful. She looks well cared for and some poor child is going to be broken-hearted if you don't do something. I don't care what it costs. I'll pay for it myself.'

My only dilemma was how to explain to my host that, having arrived for dinner, I was now leaving again. Peeping through the front window, I couldn't see anyone and quickly decided that if they didn't know I had arrived yet, I could probably get away and be back again before I was any more than fashionably late.

The little cat lay crumpled in the ditch. A few people had gathered around with the usual morbid fascination. I could immediately see that it was hopeless. Her rapid, shallow breathing was almost imperceptible. I gently checked her gums and the blanched colour, in stark contrast to the deep red blood pooled in front of her, confirmed that the tiny creature was not far from death. A shocked gasp arose from those close enough to see, as, having quickly checked for fractures, I rolled her over to see an eye protruding from its socket. This, and the awkward angle of the fractured leg drew the attention of the onlookers but, although they did not necessarily worry me unduly, the faint heartbeat and the unresponsive pupils made my mind up. There was no option but to put the little cat to sleep.

As yet, no owner had been found and while I went through the motions of further examining the shattered little body, I was trying to work out the best way of doing it. Looking up at the hopeful young faces of the children all dressed up in their Christmas best, I quickly made up my mind. Gently wrapping the cat in the blanket that one thoughtful onlooker had brought out, I turned to the lady who had phoned and told her that it would be best if I brought the cat back to the surgery. I assured her that I would let her know later how we had got on. She hurriedly scribbled down her name and number. I felt slightly guilty about the deception, even more so when I noticed one small girl clutching her big sister's hand with tears in her eyes. 'Please make her better,' she whispered as I turned away.

What a start to the day! I thought to myself, as I headed back to the surgery, in a direction that was taking me still further from my Christmas dinner. At least if I had been able to do something I wouldn't have minded, but looking at the motionless body beside me, I was quite sure that there was nothing I could do to save the animal.

The spirit of peace and goodwill evoked by the Christmas Mass had entirely evaporated as I dejectedly opened the surgery door, knowing that some child was going to have a very unhappy Christmas. I felt such a failure that I could do nothing for the little black cat on this of all days in the year.

I rang Donal to let him know I was delayed, but wouldn't be much longer.

'Oh well,' he sighed philosophically, 'why would today be any different to any other day?'

The surgery was eerily still and quiet. I carried the little bundle to the consulting table and went into the back room to fill a syringe full of the lethal agent. Gently, I unwrapped the blanket, half expecting to find the cat dead already. She was still breathing, although only just. I ran my hand down along the sleek coat, noticing the velvety red collar which, judging by its newness, might only have been put on that very morning. For a second time I took it off and examined it, hoping against hope that I might have missed a name or phone number. I don't know why I decided to put it back on her again – somehow it just seemed right. For the last time, I stroked the sleek body as I reached to pick up the syringe. I paused for a moment. And looked again. I gently laid my hand back on her chest. No! I must be imagining it. For a moment, I thought I had felt a purr from deep within. I waited for the next faint breath but there it was again. A deep rumble. Again, I ran my hand along her body and with each exhalation came the purr, growing ever so slightly louder with each breath. Quickly, I racked my brains to see was there some innate physiological reflex that caused purring with imminent death – a sort of a feline swan song – but it didn't make sense to me. I pulled out a stethoscope and placed it over the ribcage and listened intently to the faint but regular heartbeat, and, in between, the deep, throbbing rumble. As it was by now well after one o'clock, I reckoned I was most unfashionably late for dinner anyway and, somehow, I just couldn't give up on this little creature now.

It was worth a try, I decided.

I moistened a gauze swab with saline and placed it carefully over the prolapsed eyeball, having lubricated it with a viscous eye ointment. After a quick root in the surgery drawers, I pulled out the narrowest intravenous cannula I could find and clipped up the forearm. This cat desperately needed fluids – and probably lots, lots more, too, than I with my scant six months' experience could offer. Holding my breath, I clamped the leg with one hand and rapidly pumped the paw. I poked hopelessly at the shaved limb, waiting to find even a hint of a vein. Nothing. I inserted the point of the cannula, eyes fixed on the hub, hoping to see a drop of blood. Still nothing. Again, I redirected the needle. Still no blood. The little cat lay motionless. The purring had stopped now. Repeated attempts failed to locate anything that might in any way resemble a vein through which to administer the fluids which now lay heating in a sink full of hot tap water. With renewed enthusiasm, I tried the other leg. Still nothing. I tried to convince myself that it was due to the state of shock the cat was in, and that her delicate little veins had totally collapsed, but I still wondered if it was just me.

Had I not been too far away I might have taken up Paddy, from my first attempt at euthanising a dog, on his offer. Being so laid back, they might not have minded a Christmas callout.

In desperation, I removed the red collar yet again. This time I clipped some hair from the neck, hoping to find a jugular vein. So engrossed was I in the procedure, that I jumped guiltily when the phone rang, as though someone had caught me in the act of doing such a feeble job. Joyce's voice brought me back to reality with a start. I glanced at my watch and realised it was after two o'clock.

'Gillian, where are you? We're here waiting for you. Donal's been here for ages. What on earth are you doing?'

Apologising as humbly as I could, I filled her in and

asked her to go ahead without me. Judging by the merry sounds in the background, I wouldn't be missed too much anyway.

'I just hope the owners appreciate what you are doing for them,' Joyce finished, clearly indignant about the whole business. I didn't bother to fill her in on the details of the cat's present unclaimed status.

By now, the bag of fluids heating in the sink was practically boiling, so I emptied the sink and filled it with cold water, feeling slightly as though I were setting out on a merry-go-round. After a last failed stab at the elusive jugular, I decided on a new approach. Trying to recall our fluid therapy lectures in college, I could picture the page of options in the typed notes: subcutaneous (too slow), intravenous (if only), intraperitoneal – too slow as well but, at this stage, probably better than nothing.

While not an ideal option for a cat suffering from shock, I had no alternative now, so I clipped a small amount of hair from the abdomen and, having swabbed it with disinfectant, gently inserted a needle through the body wall. I hoped I had hit the right spot as I injected first one, and then a second syringe full of the now suitably cooled fluids.

The cat was still motionless. Now, no matter how hard I tried, I couldn't elicit the purr. I was beginning to wonder had I imagined it all.

Feeling disheartened, I rechecked the tiny body but, other than the eye and the broken leg, I could find no other obvious injuries – well, not obvious to me anyway. I didn't know if there was any internal bleeding or not but decided to bandage the abdomen anyway – it could do no harm.

I filled another syringe full of fluids, gently flushed out the prolapsed eye and with a fresh piece of saline-soaked gauze, I managed to clean off the pieces of dirt that had adhered to the drying organ. I placed a suture in both eyelids, wishing it was not Christmas Day and that I could call on an extra pair of hands to help. Although under normal circumstances, this procedure would be carried out under general anaesthetic, with the cat unconscious, there was no need. Using one hand to pull the eyelids apart, I used my other hand to try to ease the lubricated eye back into the empty socket with the moistened gauze swab. It took far more pressure than I had anticipated as it stubbornly slithered out first one side and then the other, obstinately refusing to go in the direction I required. I was beginning to reconsider that syringe of lethal injection when suddenly, as if by magic, the eye slotted back into the socket and, for the first time, I felt that maybe there was hope. The eye looked relatively okay but I decided to suture the lids together anyway, having applied a generous squirt of antibiotic eye ointment.

Next, I examined the leg which dangled helplessly off the blanket. After a quick examination, I thanked God that at least it was a pretty clean break and that no sharp edges had gone through the skin. However, trying to straighten the leg required a bit of effort. Slowly and carefully, I pulled the fractured end from the body, while trying with my other hand to realign the sharp edges. As I did so, a sudden deep yowl came from the cat and she pulled her leg against me. Despite her obvious pain, I was delighted to get some reaction. Initially, I had been afraid to give her any further medication but now I injected more painkillers, frustrated that I didn't have access to a vein to allow them to work more rapidly. Another rummage through the presses revealed an assortment of bandages and some plaster of Paris that would do to cast the leg. Having soaked the casting material in some warm water, I applied it as best I could, hoping that the realigned ends of the fractured radius would stay in place until it set. After a few minutes, the cast was nice and hard and I started the laborious task of cleaning up the mess.

The cat was now quiet again, and her breathing seemed easier than before. Her pale membranes still scared me though.

By this stage, I decided that I was so late anyway I might as well have a last try for the elusive vein.

Pulling out yet another cannula from its sterile sheath, I stretched out the cat's neck and placed my finger deep into the groove where the vein should have been. But to no avail – try as I might, I couldn't feel anything. Hopelessly, I poked the point of the cannula into the general area of the vein, redirecting it again and again. Just as I was about to give up again, a little bubble of blood appeared in the hub and I held my breath, afraid to move in case the sharp tip of the stylet would pierce through the fragile, collapsing vein. Ever so slowly, I advanced the plastic cannula, gradually withdrawing the metal stylet, and, still holding my breath, watched as the drop of blood on the hub slowly enlarged and finally dropped on to the cat's neck. I felt like dancing for joy but contained myself in case it all fell out. Then I realised that the giving set – the plastic tubing that connects the bag of fluids to the intravenous cannula – which I had left ready to hand, had by now made its way over to the far side of the table. This meant that I had to balance precariously on one leg still holding the line in place, while stretching over with the other hand, to retrieve the errant giving set with the tip of my finger. Having finally attached it to the bag of fluids, I released the valve and then cursed as nothing happened – until I saw the kink in the tubing. Once readjusted, the fluids ran in freely.

Happy at last, I sutured the cannula in place, determined that it wouldn't come out again. Drawing from the depths of my memory of six months previously in college, I tried to recall the formula for the shock rate of fluids for a cat. Having hooked the fluid bag off a conveniently located press handle, I again began to stroke the black fur. And there it was – the deep-throated purr. Time blurred as I stood there, stroking the cat's body in time with the purr, almost hypnotising myself, whatever about the cat.

Eventually, I dragged myself away. There was nothing more I could do. Although I doubted it, the colour of the cat's gums did seem to be improving and, as I checked the reflexes in her unsutured eye, she started to paddle her paws.

Having done what I could, I suddenly remembered my neglected stomach and the smell of roast turkey that had been wafting out from Joyce's porch. With the cat tucked up in a small cage, I fished in my pocket for the torn piece of paper and dialled the number of the lady who had rung me in the first place.

Soon I was back at Joyce's house in an atmosphere of Christmas cheer and doing justice to the huge plate of dinner that had been kept warming in the oven for me, not caring if the gravy was the only thing keeping it moist.

Joyce seemed bewildered by the whole situation.

'I'd kill her if I was you,' she kept repeating to Donal as her wine glass teetered dangerously close to the edge of the arm rest. Luckily, both he and Greg were engrossed in an old video of a hurling final, and were oblivious to all else.

It was five o'clock before I managed to haul myself back out of the chair and return to the surgery, not daring to think what I would do if it had all been a waste of time. Donal came with me this time and I was glad to have some moral support as I braced myself for the worst.

The little cat was sitting up looking decidedly perky although the right eye was slightly glazed. I waited as I ran my hand along her back and although she quivered as I touched over some areas of bruising, by the second stroke, I could detect her regular purr. She sat uncomplainingly as I examined the cast leg and listened to a heart which was now much stronger and more audible. Another quick examination revealed nothing further, other than a full bladder – which meant that at least the organ was probably still intact.

Miraculously, by Stephen's Day morning, she was up and walking around, daintily holding up the injured limb. She purred with an almost tiger-like growl as she wolfed down the leftover turkey I had brought her.

I finished my locum stint that night and left a note for Bill outlining the details and leaving him a number for the lady.

Despite my being sure that the cat had an owner, as yet none had turned up. I was beginning to get worried, but having a long drive home, I had no option but to leave her where she was. Her purrs as I said goodbye seemed extra throaty, as though she knew.

I tried to put her out of my mind, which wasn't too difficult as I joined a busy three-vet practice in Wicklow with Christmas lambs and calving heifers. An exceptionally good summer and mild autumn had left a lot of them in too good a condition, with oversized calves in fat cows, and it was here that I did my first two Caesareans.

About three weeks later, a letter arrived that had been forwarded from Bill's practice. As I slit it open, out fell a picture of a sleek-looking, glossy black cat, with a red velvet collar, being cuddled affectionately in the arms of a young girl.

The attached note began: 'Dear Christmas Day Vet'. It was from the owner. She had turned up the morning after I had left, overjoyed to find the little animal alive and well. Ebony, as the cat was called, had made a full recovery, she said, and was now purring even louder than ever before.

If only they knew how that purring had probably saved her life.

MIXED-ANIMAL PRACTICE IN WICKLOW

CHAPTER TWELVE

A DESPERATE CASE

It was eight o'clock by the time I had finished the evening surgery and I still had one more call to do. A farmer had rung to say that he had a cow with a prolapsed uterus. I was only a week into my new job in the heart of Wicklow and this was my first evening on call by myself. Although Riverdale Veterinary Clinic was a mixed-animal practice, as it was now coming into spring it seemed to be largely taken over by the cattle and sheep work.

'Give us a ring if you need a hand with anything,' Seamus, the boss, had offered, on his way out that afternoon.

A prolapse in a sheep is rectified easily enough but in a cow, when the whole uterus or calf bed is forced out, it's not so easy. I had seen experienced vets struggle with such cases, and wondered how I myself would fare as it would be the first time I would attempt to replace one. I hesitated for a moment, wondering if I should ring Seamus, for the cow's sake as much as for my own, but then decided against it. After all, I didn't want to look like a total waster in my first week.

Twenty minutes later, I was standing in a small, dark shed on the top of the hillside, observing my patient. The cow was stretched out, eyes rolling in her head, moaning softly to herself. As I became accustomed to the darkness, I shuddered to see the enormous, red, bulging mass protruding from her rear end. Somehow I didn't remember the ones I had seen during my student years ever looking quite as big or as swollen as this one.

It looked as if it might have happened some time ago. John, the farmer, had been away on holidays and had left a neighbour checking the stock, so it was hard to be sure exactly what had happened.

As I tried to mentally rearrange the cow into a more suitable position, my mind flitted back to my final-year oral exam when I had confidently explained how to sedate the cow, administer an epidural and then roll her over to pull the two hind legs out behind her in a froglike position. I discussed in great detail how I would then cradle the neat little prolapsed organ on a sheet of spotlessly clean plastic. I had further explained the importance of pushing it back in, gently yet firmly, with the palm of the hands, taking great care not to use the fingers least they rupture the delicate organ.

I was very proud of my honours degree in reproduction but now I felt that a bit more practical experience would have been a lot more help than the neatly framed piece of paper.

I immediately decided to forget about the sedation bit. It looked as though even the tiniest bit would be enough to push the cow over the edge, and, I didn't think that the collapsed form in the straw was going to put up much of a fight anyway. Instead, I decided to go for a hefty dose of intravenous steroid and some calcium borogluconate, hoping that they might improve her chances of survival. While I set about scrubbing and clipping the site for the epidural, I sent John to arrange a bit more light.

Normally, a floppy tail indicates that the epidural has hit the spot, but this one was floppy before I had even injected her. I would have to wait until I started to work on the prolapse to see if she would strain against me. Although the cow was totally unresisting, it took three of us to heave her dead weight around to get her in a position that would allow me a bit of space to work under the flash lamps that John had organised.

It took longer than I expected to gently wash and remove all the bits of dirt and straw and the semi-rotted pieces of the placenta that still adhered to the uterus, but the time passed quickly enough as I chatted to John and his neighbour, subconsciously trying to put off the inevitable moment when I would have to start the real work. They were both young farmers and I was glad to have pleasant company and a bit of extra muscle power for the job. I could have done with some sugar to pour on the calf bed because by now, having been out for some time, the prolapsed organ had become grossly oedematous, which was going to add to my troubles getting it back in. Sugar has an amazing ability to draw out a lot of the fluid by simple osmosis, but when I realised that the house was a good half mile from the yard, I decided to make do without it.

Finally, I could put off the inevitable moment no longer and I started to push, remembering to use only the palm of my hands as indicated in our college lectures. I knelt behind the cow, cradling the engorged uterus on a piece of grubby, well-used silage plastic, supported on either side by John and his neighbour. Placing the palms of my hands around the edges of the mass, I pushed ... and pushed ... and pushed even harder until I could feel myself going red in the face.

Nothing happened.

I smiled confidently at the two men, rearranged my position and pushed again ... and again ... and again.

Still nothing happened.

I don't know how long this went on for until I had to take a break. I sat back to look at it and said, as much to myself as to the farmers: 'I think it's getting smaller.'

'Definitely!' said one.

'Absolutely!' the other.

Once I had caught my breath, I started again, this time concentrating on the underneath part. I thought I had pro-gressed by a few centimetres until I noticed that it had all come back out at the top end. Both farmers jumped sud-denly in response to the string of curses that broke out of me. I think until that point they had thought I was refined and ladylike, despite the job.

'Sorry,' I mumbled, as they both stared at me.

'Not at all, curse all you like if it helps,' John replied politely.

Another ten minutes of unsuccessful pushing went by, during which they were exposed to the full range of my expletives as I forced and strained against the fragile uterus, trying not to put my hand through it. My college oral seemed a million miles away and by now, I was desperately pushing with palms, fingers, elbows, knees and anything else that I could call into play.

My arms ached and my legs were paining with the effort of supporting the uncooperative mass of tissue. No matter how hard I tried to convince myself that I was making progress, it still looked no smaller. I sat back and stripped off my jacket and sweatshirt and envied the male vets who, when in need, could discard all of their upper garments.

I was starting to feel a lot sorrier for myself than for the unfortunate cow and I was amazed to hear the farmers muttering sympathetic things like: 'You must be exhausted by now. Come on up for a cup of tea. Sure there was nothing you could have done anyway.'

The prospect of having to give up on the animal and admit failure gave me a renewed surge of energy and determination. I set to work again, with a just a slight edge of frantic desperation.

I had gone past the point of pain by the time I looked down and, to my immense relief, saw that this time the thing really was getting smaller. Both farmers had gone silent but you could almost feel the renewed hope in the air. Ten minutes later and it was by now about the size of a normal prolapse, even though over half of it had gone back in. I worked unrelentingly at the last portion and, with a feeling of disbelief, I watched as the last section was sucked back into the vagina. In a daze, I followed it in until my arm was in past the shoulder and I pushed the two horns of the uterus back into their rightful positions.

If I was expecting a round of applause from the cow I was wasting my time: she lay, head sunk to the ground, apparently uncaring of her fate. John, however, was very appreciative of my efforts and thanked me profusely – a nice change from the tirades of abuse to which vets may sometimes be subjected if the job has taken too long.

It was only when he said to me: 'We were lucky to get you tonight. I reckon your boss would just have shot her,' that a niggling doubt started to creep into my mind. Seamus was, after all, a lot more experienced than I was and, in all my student years, I had never seen such a bad case as this one. I quickly dismissed the thoughts from my mind. Right now I felt as though I myself was going to die, and I certainly couldn't cope if the cow did too, after all my efforts.

Working in slow motion, I placed a big Buehner's suture around the vulva, wondering if it would be a waste of time if she decided to force again but at least it made me feel better. All that was left to do was to give her a shot of anti-biotics – the rest was up to her.

When I got home, I relayed my story to Donal and we sat up for a while, unwinding over a few cans. When I finally made it to bed that night, the dull throbbing in my muscles, unaccustomed to the day's exertions, prevented me from sleeping. I tossed and turned and couldn't help wondering how my patient was faring.

I knew it was a sign of inexperience but at nine o'clock

the next morning, I just had to ring John to find out how she was getting on. I sincerely hoped that she was feeling better than I was. My heart thumped as I waited for the phone to be answered.

John's voice was muted. 'I really appreciate what you did for her last night.'

'That's no problem at all, but how is she now?' I interrupted.

'She died an hour ago.'

Suddenly the pains in my arms and legs doubled. I realised that my lack of experience had put not only myself but also the cow through an unnecessary ordeal. I should have shot her.

It seemed that fate was mocking me as in the weeks that followed I was inundated with calls to attend prolapsed cows. I have never seen one as bad as John's cow since but, as my muscles toughened up and became accustomed to the hard labour, at least I knew that if I had managed to get that one back in, I would never fail again.

CHAPTER THIRTEEN

SIDNEY GOES HOME

As always when confronted with a problem in my first year as a vet, my mind flashed back to my student experiences and what I had learned in the lab. It seemed like only the other day that we had stood over the dissection tables in our white coats, gulping slightly as the faint odour of not-so-fresh flesh assailed our nostrils. Not that the smell was in any way unusual to us at this stage of our training but, combined with the after-effects of the previous night's drinking session, it was all just a bit too much. Our task for this practical was to first remove a section of intestine and then to surgically re-appose the cut ends, in preparation for the day when a real live patient might present with an obstruction in such an advanced state that the gut itself might have become necrotic and need to be removed. Sitting in the surgical lab, such a real-life scenario seemed a long, long way away.

Gingerly, my colleague and I, both looking equally ashen-faced and hungover, incised the smooth lining of the section of intestine lying on the table in front of us. We watched as the muscle layers below bulged out to meet us, neither of us either remembering or caring for their official titles, as the dog to whom they had once belonged had long since departed on his journey to the great doggy heaven in the sky. Trying hard to summon up some enthusiasm for the task, I methodically placed a pair of stay sutures at either side of the diameter of the gut, hands shaking slightly as I fiddled with the tiny round-bodied needle that the professor had reliably informed us would be less traumatic. Slowly, I began to reunite the gut with a series of minute sutures, no more than two millimetres apart. The aim was to apply the correct degree of tension to ensure an adequate seal without occluding what, in a live dog, would be the healing supply of blood vessels. Normally I enjoyed these practical surgery sessions but today, as waves of nausea swept over me and my head pounded, I wearily handed over the needle to my colleague who had long since lost interest.

'Here, you have a go.'

Reluctantly, she pulled herself up from where she lay slumped over the table beside me. Gradually, as she stitched, the sutures became further and further apart as her enthusiasm waned.

'Do you think that would do?' she enquired as she held out the completed section of intestine before me.

'Emmm, well, I suppose it might – as long as he hadn't chewed his food too well,' I giggled as I poked a forceps between the sutures that were supposedly rejoining the gut.

But today was no laughing matter.

Today, I was a fully-qualified veterinary surgeon and the section of necrotic gut belonged to a very affable and very much alive Springer Spaniel with an unfortunate liking for rubbish bins. Today my shaking hands and the waves of nausea were a million miles from a hangover: they were purely stress-induced.

*   *   *

It had all started late the night before as I lay in bed assuring myself that it was going to be a quiet night. I had developed a habit of staying awake until midnight when I was on call as this was the time when most calls seemed to come in. It somehow never seemed quite as bad to have to get up, even if you had gone to bed, once you were still awake. Normally, once you hit midnight, most of your clients were in bed too, although it didn't always work out like that. Even so, your chances of getting a decent night's sleep were better.

Just as I began to doze off, the phone rang. Twelve-twenty flashed the clock by the bedside.

Half an hour later, I was down in the surgery where a very dejected-looking Springer Spaniel, called Sidney, lay prostrate on the table in front of me.

'Are you sure he was okay when you went out?' I questioned Jacqui, his owner, whose hastily thrown-on raincoat couldn't disguise the glamour beneath – much more suited to the night out on the town that she had come from.

'Well, now that you mention it, he has been a bit quiet

for the last few days, but I thought maybe he was just starting to get a bit of sense.'

I didn't air my doubts, remembering the last time Sidney had visited the surgery when he had tried to jump out a four-foot high window, taking with him two cat baskets – complete with spitting felines – which, by some trick of nature understood only by a Springer Spaniel, had managed to become entangled in his lead.

'Yes, I'm just thinking now … He hasn't really eaten much for the past few days either.'

'Any vomiting?'

'Oh, of course,' she groaned, 'how could I have forgotten? You see, we'd just bought this new carpet for the living room and the very next day when I came home, well, I couldn't even think about it now …' she continued, hands clutched over her mouth as though she were going to repeat the actions of her luckless dog.

At this hour of the night my sympathy was at its lowest ebb and I tried to hurry her up a bit.

'Right so,' I carried on briskly, running my hands over Sidney's swollen abdomen. 'What colour was it?'

'What colour? Of course. Yes, well it's a lovely delicate shade of peach, with just the slightest tint of silver running through it.'

I stared at her incredulously for a few moments, until it struck me. 'I meant the vomit, Jacqui, not the carpet,' I replied wearily.

Having ascertained that it was 'a nasty-looking colour', a detail that I didn't bother to write down in my clinical notes, and that she had no idea if he had vomited again since she had kept him outside to make amends for his misdemeanour, I carried on.

'Is he passing his droppings normally?'

'Oh,' she gasped, as though I had asked her about some of the more intimate details of her own private life, 'I've no idea. Derek deals with all that sort of thing.'

I felt a momentary pang of sympathy for her husband whom I had met on the previous occasion. He struck me as having a slightly henpecked air about him. Still, at least he appeared to be genuinely fond of the dog.

I didn't know whether it was Jacqui's fault or mine at this late hour of the night but, somehow, we just didn't seem to be getting through to each other. I gave up all hope of taking any sort of a sensible history and carried on with a thorough clinical examination instead. I observed the dark, purple-tinged mucous membranes, the sunken eyes and inelastic coat and the bloated abdomen that flinched as I palpated a specific point. It was all too obvious what the problem was.

'I'm afraid Sidney has a blockage. He'll more than likely need surgery but he's in no condition to be operated on tonight.'

Far from being distraught, Jacqui paid scant attention to my explanations and happily left him with me, clearly relieved that she did not have to take him home with her.

Grateful to be finally left on my own to get on with the job, I placed a bag of fluid in the microwave and clipped up Sidney's forearm. He didn't even flinch as I inserted the cannula into the vein. Then I attached the giving set through which the fluids would infuse overnight, in preparation for surgery the next day.

'Now, you get a good night's sleep, Sid,' I told him as I injected a gut-relaxing drug and some antibiotics. 'We've got a big day ahead of us tomorrow.'

Just how big a day it was going to be seemed to expand and enlarge in my mind as I slept fitfully through the night, frequently waking to find myself mid-op, gouging out never-ending lengths of rotted gut, which seemed to increase and multiply as I pulled. Luckily, I was still dreaming at that stage.

Sidney appeared a little brighter and cheerfully flopped his tail at me the next morning. In vain hope, I checked the day's appointment book to find that both Seamus and Arthur, the other assistant, would be tied up testing cattle for the rest of the morning. I had half-hoped to fob Sidney off on one of them, although neither was particularly interested in small-animal work. There was nothing for it but to start scrubbing up the selection of instruments that I would need for the surgery. Niamh, the nurse, appeared not to notice my air of distractedness as she filled me in on her social plans for the weekend. My monosyllabic replies didn't deter her in the least.

All too soon, I was incising into the carefully clipped and scrubbed abdomen and, as the stench of decomposing gut hit me, I was for a moment back in my surgical practical, except that this time the dog was alive – so far.

The blocked gut was immediately obvious as a bulging, blackened mass protruded from my tidy incision. Hesitantly, I clamped either end of the lesion and excised all the unhealthy looking tissue, trying as best I could to prevent any intestinal fluid from oozing into the depths of the abdomen. Having removed the piece of necrotic gut, I opened up the section which now lay on my surgical tray. I couldn't help laughing as I discovered the offending object – a very well-chewed heel of a stiletto shoe.

'Oh Sidney,' I said to the sleeping dog. 'I just hope they were very expensive!'

Just as I was trying to figure out which part of the blood supply I was trying to cut off and which part I was trying to maintain, Niamh decided to take an interest in the proceedings.

'Oh vomit!' she said, wrinkling up her nose at the mess sitting on the table. 'You know her husband's a solicitor, don't you? Imagine if he dies!'

'I'd rather not,' I replied dryly, as yet another stitch pulled through the fragile intestine.

My eyes were beginning to boggle by the time I had inserted what I thought might be a sufficient number of tiny sutures to re-appose the gut. I tried not to think of our professor back in the practical, clamping either end of the re-attached gut into which he then injected water, and his disdainful face as the fluid seeped out through at least five gaps in the supposedly repaired intestine. Why, oh why hadn't we tried a bit harder?

Gently, I pulled out a large fold of the glistening omentum in which the body organs are suspended and wrapped it around the section of gut, willing it to fulfil its healing role and soak up any leaks from my inexperienced repair.

I left Sidney comfortably tucked up in a large cage under a heat lamp and, by the time I got back from my morning rounds, he was sitting up. Considering that he'd had half his insides spread out on the operating table not two hours previously, I thought he looked well.

'We'll have to keep him on fluids for the first few days,' I explained to Jacqui when I finally caught up with her that evening. She obviously wasn't so concerned as to have been sitting by the phone awaiting my call all afternoon.

'Could you not just keep him in for the week until he's over it all?' she begged, despite my protests that this really would not be necessary. 'You see, I've such a busy schedule at the moment – it is regatta week you know.'

'Well, if that's what you want.'

In one way, I was glad to have Sid around over the next few days as I gradually reintroduced solid food and observed with relief the first few squirts of faeces which were at least a sign that things were moving in the right direction. But I knew that things could still go wrong. At night, my dreams were filled with images of leaking intestines and sludgy brown liquid insidiously oozing over a peach-coloured carpet. However, by day, Sidney improved dramatically and, by early the next week, he had deposited proof of his full recovery in the shape of a perfectly formed solid dump in the run outside. I rang Jacqui to tell her the good news.

'He's pulled through one hundred percent. Not a bother on him. You can take him home as soon as you're ready.'

Although I wasn't expecting the ecstatic reply with which one is occasionally rewarded by a grateful client, I couldn't believe my ears when she dropped her bombshell.

'Well, that's lovely. You're marvellous really,' she

gushed, 'but, well, it's a bit awkward really. To be honest, it's been so peaceful without him around the house that really, I think it would be best if you could find a new home for him. We will fix up your bill, of course.'

'What a waste, after all your work,' declared Niamh as I relayed the gist of the conversation. 'What a bloody waste.'

But no, I thought to myself, as I stroked the unfortunate Sidney's silky ears. At least the important part had worked out. After all he had been through, there was no way I was putting Sid to sleep despite Jacqui's interjection of 'Well, whatever you feel you must do' when I tried to play on her conscience by telling her that I might have to put him down.

Ten days later, as I waved off Mr and Mrs Jemison, newly arrived in the area having relocated from Wales, I was very glad for Sidney that Jacqui had got bored with his high spirits. The minute they came through the surgery door with a hesitant 'We were wondering if you knew of any big dog looking for a good home ...' I knew they were perfect. Two boisterous lads tumbled in behind them and chimed in: 'Yeah, we want a really big dog!'

Having discovered that they had bought a house in the next village on two acres and enjoyed long evening walks and trips to the mountains every weekend, I introduced them. It was love at first sight.

Sidney, back to his old self, managed to pull down an entire rack of information leaflets with him as he bounced out the door taking a flying leap over an elderly and bewildered-looking Westie that had been sitting quietly with his owner. Just this once, I decided I could forgive him.

CHAPTER FOURTEEN

A DYING BREED

It was one of those days when working with large animals seemed to be the best job in the world. Not for me being stuck in a musty office, staring with glazed eyes at a computer screen. Not for me the slow crawl through the snake-like rush-hour traffic to the crowded city centre. I grinned smugly to myself as the jeep made its way up the meandering roadways, high up into the snowy Wicklow mountains.

'Mrs Trooper, Ballybreathnach – lame bullock' read the note in my daybook.

I hadn't been to this particular farm before but I knew that Mrs Trooper was an elderly widow whose husband had died the previous Christmas, leaving her to manage the smallholding with the help of an equally ancient brother-in-law. I contemplated how, sadly, in a few short years, this breed of hill farmer would have all but died out, to be substituted by the large, impersonal, intensive farms.

As I pulled into the lopsided driveway, Mrs Trooper

came bustling out from the kitchen doorway, busily brushing down a floury apron. She dragged open the rickety gate before I could get to it.

'Well, I'm that sorry to be dragging you out on a bitter day like this,' she began as I stepped out of the car. 'Sure, you'll come in for a quick cup before we go up to look at Hubert,' she continued, leading me into the kitchen. I gasped at the blast of heat that met me at the doorway and soon my toes began to tingle as I perched myself up against the big Aga in the corner. A warm glow enveloped me as the old lady fussed around, pouring out mugs of tea.

'Sure, you must be worn out,' she said, peering up at me, 'a little thing like you doing a man's job.'

I had long since given up trying to convert that generation of hill farmers to the concept of a female vet and couldn't help smiling to myself as I thought of this morning's jobs; a two-day-old calf with scour, a tom-cat neuter and a nanny-goat with a cough – no wonder I needed a strong cup of tea to brace myself after such demands.

Reluctantly, I drained the last of my cup, as Alfred, the brother-in-law, made his appearance, his robust frame in stark contrast to that of frail Mrs Trooper. He insisted on taking the durable box that contained my hoof instruments from me as I pulled it out of the back of the jeep.

As we made our way across the snow-covered yard, I was slightly alarmed to see the shed in the distance. It seemed to be far, far away, tucked into the side of a steep ditch. Although it looked very old and had been well-weathered over the years, it must have been a fine shed in its day. I was amazed at the speed with which Mrs Trooper made her way up the snowy banks, and I had to concentrate on keeping up with her without losing my balance. For a brief instant, she reminded me of a mountain goat as she deftly picked her way over the rough banks.

'Hubert was the last calf we got out of Hilda. I remember well the night he was born – not long before George died, Lord rest his soul. That one never threw a calf but that we had a tough pull out of her. Never had need for a vet, though. Our George, Lord rest his soul, surely was a man to calve a cow.

'"Franny," he used say to me, "it'll be a long night. You may as well leave the kettle on the stove." I used to worry about him, so I did, as he got older. He had a bad cough there for a while, but wasting my time I was with him trying to get him to see a doctor.

'There was a mighty wind the night Hubert was born,' she continued as she hauled open the wooden gate that led into the shed. 'I don't know which was worse, the noise of the wind rattling through the roof or the coughing of George, Lord rest his soul. "Will I go down and ring the vet?" said I to him a second time. "Neither my father before me nor I ever had need of a vet to calve a cow and I won't be starting now." And that was the end of it. Well, he's gone now and here you are!' she finished and then paused for a moment, clearly remembering the years gone by. I was glad of this interlude as it allowed me to catch my breath before pulling up the overalls that were hanging around my waist.

Once my eyes had become accustomed to the subdued light in the shed after the glare of the bright, snowy fields, the sight that greeted me was a pleasant one. It was full of the sweet smell of hay-fed beasts, bedded on good wheaten straw, the silence punctuated only by a contented chewing of the cud as the animals stared quizzically at my unexpected entrance. For all the advances of science and modern agricultural methods, I thought to myself, there was a lot to be said for the old ways.

It was easy enough to pick out my patient for the day. In contrast to his comrades, he stood in obvious discomfort, holding a fore-limb just short of the ground.

'He was right as rain yesterday when I threw them in their bit of fodder,' cut in Alfred, anxious to have his say before his sister-in-law got going again, 'but first thing this morning, I noticed he couldn't put his claw down. I tried to have a look at it but the auld divil won't stand still for me.'

'George, Lord rest his soul, was a right man to repair a foot in his day,' Mrs Trooper remarked wistfully.

She continued to regale me with stories of different animals they had nursed through a variety of ailments over the years. I tied my rope above Hubert's knee and, after a quick investigation, found a nearby plank to tie it on to, in order to winch up his leg. It was a rare farm nowadays that didn't have a crush but the bullock seemed quiet enough as I squeezed the claws with my hoof testers, until a sudden indignant bellow confirmed my suspicion. After a quick hunt through my hoof-box, I pulled out a glistening new hoof-knife and, despite my awkward handling of the unfamiliar instrument, was rewarded with a spurt of pus as I drained my first ever foot abscess.

'Well, I never!' exclaimed Mrs Trooper as the flow of infection slowed to a trickle.

'How in the Lord's name could that have happened and him on a good straw bed?'

'Oh, sure, you know yourself what they're like,' I replied. 'He must have got a prod one of the days and then the infection would have eventually built up in him.'

I couldn't help noticing the obvious culprit – a worn plank that had broken loose and had a few rusty nails sticking out at the base, but I wasn't going to mention it to the elderly pair. I was happy that Alfred would have no trouble bathing the foot in a hot solution of Epsom salts for a few days, 'and then he'll be right as rain,' I reassured them.

When Mrs Trooper went ahead to heave open the heavy timber gate, I hastily turned over the loose plank and kicked it in under the divide where it could cause no further damage.

As I stood in the spotless little washroom off Mrs Trooper's warm kitchen, scrubbing my hands with the well-used bar of soap, a mouth-watering smell began to waft in from the next room. Although it was still before noon, the fresh crispness of the morning was beginning to work on my appetite.

'Take your time in there,' she called out to me, 'and I'll have a few sausages on a plate for you in a minute.'

'Not at all,' I replied half-heartedly, 'sure didn't I just have a cup of tea!'

'Now, they're there on the pan for you, Gillian, and you couldn't see them going to waste,' she replied firmly.

I didn't argue with her.

By the time I was respectable, the table had miraculously become laden with home-made brown bread, a slab of cheddar cheese and a pot of blackberry jam. In the middle of this spread was a plate piled high not only with the sausages but also rashers, fried eggs, black and white pudding, tomatoes and a home-made potato cake.

'George, Lord rest his soul, did enjoy his bit of grub. Never lost his appetite until the day he died. The pan was still soaking in the sink when he passed away. Alfred takes a bite up in his own house now so there's not much need for me to be cooking anymore.'

While I ate, Mrs Trooper reminisced about her farming days – about how she had married into the small-holding in her early twenties, through the years when the rearing of her two sons and her daughter occupied her time along with the hundred and one never-ending chores to be carried out on the farm.

'They've all moved on now,' she finished, topping up my mug with steaming, fresh tea. 'Two in Dublin and one in Galway, all married with families of their own, thank God.'

'Were you sorry none of them stayed on to farm?' I questioned cautiously.

'Lord no!' she replied firmly, 'although with the help of God I'll live my days out in it. We loved the farm and the life that went with it, though it was always a struggle. We brought them up well on it but I'm happy to see them move on. Young people expect more from life now than what this farm could provide for.'

And yet, I thought to myself as I carefully drove back down the icy country roads, will they be any better off in their high-tech careers, working harder to meet the demands of living harder? And will their own children have the same contented upbringing?

The demands of my own job kept me busy for the next while and I had all but forgotten the call until I saw another entry in the book a month or so later.

'Mrs Trooper, Ballybreathnach – blood test cows.'

That's strange, I thought to myself. Cows were usually only tested on their annual herd test, which, in her case, was not due for another few months, or if they were going for sale, but surely she had nothing to sell at this time of year?

'Are you sure that's right?' I enquired of Niamh who was busily sorting through a ream of cattle cards.

'Yeah, did you not hear? The old lady had a stroke a few weeks ago. She's gone to live in a nursing home. The family has put the house and farm on the market and are selling off the stock.'

All the way up, I felt a deep pang of sadness for a lady I had met only once but who, just a few short weeks before, had sat in her homely kitchen, calmly telling me that she would live out her days on the farm. I just couldn't imagine her sitting in a room surrounded by strangers, a million miles away from the way of life she treasured. I thought of the meal she had prepared for me and wondered if it had been the last meal she had prepared for anyone.

The weather seemed to match my spirits: the bright crispness on the day of my previous visit was now replaced by squally winds and driving rain. This time I hauled open the rickety gate myself and, as I saw no sign of life in the house, made my way straight on up to the shed, coughing several times to catch my breath against the wind.

I couldn't help noticing that a number of the cattle had empty water buckets in front of them and, in contrast to the last time, the concrete floors of the stalls had only a sparse sprinkling of sodden straw. Hubert, my old patient, now seemed to have fully recovered. He eyed me watchfully as I walked past him to where the cows stood. Within minutes, I had drawn blood from the few remaining stall-tied cattle and was packing up to leave when a voice called out.

'Sorry I'm late. I was at an important meeting in Dublin and got delayed. I'm Brian – Mrs Trooper's son,' he added, holding out a hand, looking slightly conspicuous in his suit and gleaming wellies.

'I'm so sorry to hear about your mother,' I began awkwardly. 'How is she?'

'She's doing just fine,' he assured me in a smooth voice. 'It was only a minor stroke. She's recovered well, thank God. Maybe in the end it was just as well. We worried about her on her own all the time since my father died. She had this crazy notion that she would stay up here on her own but now that she's had this stroke, we've made our minds up. She's getting the best of care. A very nice nursing home in Dalkey. Costs an arm and a leg, of course, but still, it's for the best.'

A few weeks later, I saw a death notice in *The Irish Times*: 'Trooper (née Foley), Frances, (Late of Ballybreathnach, Co. Wicklow). Died peacefully in the Convent Garden Rest Home, Dalkey. Sadly missed by her loving sons, daughter and grandchildren. May she rest in peace.'

CHAPTER FIFTEEN

A TALE OF
TWO SHEEP

If I ever had to make a choice between all the domestic animals, what I would least like to be is a sheep. Although there are some notable exceptions, in general sheep tend to fare much less favourably than their bovine counterparts due to their considerably lesser individual value. And whenever market prices fall, things only get worse.

The first spring that I spent working in Riverdale Veterinary Clinic with Seamus and Arthur, things were particularly hard. Armed with an academic knowledge of sheep medicine and, to a lesser extent, of sheep surgery, I prepared myself for the onslaught of the lambing season – only to be disappointed. In a climate where the subsidy was worth more than the animal which, in turn, was worth less than the cost of a vet's visit, I found that my sheep experience remained scanty. There has to be something wrong with any system where it is more economically viable to let an animal 'take its chances' rather than help it along the way. At times it was sickening, especially in some of the bigger yards, to see animals in need of attention that they were never going to get.

Generally speaking, vets were only called in for flock health problems. Even in these cases, the problem often related back to economic issues. Basic husbandry tasks which previously would have been diligently carried out by any self-respecting stockman, were now being ignored in the hope of saving a few cent from the ever-narrowing margins. The wet winter that accompanied my arrival on the agricultural scene only exacerbated the problem.

In one such case, I was faced with a flock of ewes which was due to lamb. The farmer had noticed that they were losing condition, but several had died before a visit was deemed necessary. As the farmer herded them in, I couldn't help noticing what an unhealthy flock they were. Despite the short distance travelled, they were already quite out of breath by the time they made it to the holding pen. Even from my vantage point, I could clearly make out the classic jowl oedema in quite a few of them. I cornered one of the worst-looking ewes to examine the mucous membranes in her mouth which were pale, as I expected. The sunken eyes and the bony frame said it all.

'They have fluke,' I said to Brendan, the farmer, as he arrived with his last batch. 'Have they been dosed for it this year?'

'No, I didn't do them at all, to be honest. With the bad prices last year, and the cost of the drenches, I let it go. I don't see how it could be fluke all the same. My family are farming this spot for generations and we've never had an outbreak that I remember.'

I had to carry out a post-mortem examination on one of the ewes to convince him. The tracts in the liver were indisputable, as were the leaf-like adult fluke.

'Well, I'm amazed!' he said. 'I've never come across the likes of it before.'

'You're not the only one to be caught out this year,' I assured him. 'The combination of the wet weather and farmers having to cut back on dosing has done a lot of damage.'

He gloomily reported to me the next time I saw him that he had lost a few more, despite the treatment. I wasn't surprised – the advanced state of the disease in his flock was more than modern medicine could cure.

As a student, I had spent a few Easter holidays working on sheep farms in preparation for the years ahead. I think I lambed more ewes as a student than I have done to this day as a qualified vet. I had really enjoyed the work while still in college but once I qualified, it all changed. Most farmers were fairly handy at the job themselves, so the cases we saw were the real no-hopers; the ones when all else had failed.

After a while, it got so bad that I couldn't face eating lamb anymore. The stench of dead, decomposing lambs has a tendency to cling to you no matter what attempts you make to remove it.

The other problem with sheep was that they were so unpredictable. With my limited experience, I found it hard to say which ones would live and which would die. Obviously, the farmers could not afford to pay for treatment for a hopeless case, but on more than one occasion, the sheep had me well fooled. The only thing that was certain about them was that, despite their outward tough appearance, they didn't tolerate rough handling.

*   *   *

On the way home for dinner one evening, I wasn't overjoyed to get a call to Paul Richardson's yard to lamb a pedigree ewe. I had attended calls in Paul's yard on a couple of occasions and knew instantly that there was trouble ahead.

When I arrived in the yard, one look at the collapsed, panting ewe in the corner confirmed my suspicion. I didn't bother with the usual trivialities. I knew they would be wasted on this particular client.

'How long had she been lambing, Paul?' I asked, barely able to conceal my disgust.

'Ah, not long now. Not long at all,' he assured me.

'Since early morning at least by the look of her,' I retorted, cutting him off.

'Ah, well now, I wouldn't say that at all.'

A quick feel inside the ewe confirmed it all: her cervix was tight, only just allowing me to place the tips of my fingers in through it. Ringwomb is a common condition where despite advanced labour the cervix doesn't dilate, preventing any further progress. At the bottom of the cervix, I could feel the torn tissues where Paul had obviously forced a rough hand through the narrow passageway. Inside, the womb was dry and sticky, as all the fluids had long since drained away. By the look of the ewe, she had had about as much hardship as she could take. I knew that no matter what happened, Paul would blame me. It wouldn't for one minute occur to him that his own fumbling around inside her, tearing her with his rough hands and leaving it until the last possible minute to call a vet, could have anything to do with it.

Sadly, caesarean sections, so commonplace in cattle, are less frequently carried out in sheep as the cost of the surgery would often be greater than the value of the unfortunate ewe, especially in a case like this where her breeding potential would now be compromised.

'She's in a bad way, Paul. She's torn inside and the lamb is long dead. I don't know if she'll even pull through herself. Maybe it would be better to put her to sleep now.'

'Ah, now,' he said dismissively, 'there's not that much astray with her. Sure, 'tis only a small little lamb in her. I had a quick feel myself, you know, and I'd have had it out in no time only I'd to go off to get a puncture fixed on the tractor.'

'Right so, that's fine then,' I replied coldly as I stood up, pulled off my long lambing gloves and climbed out over the pen. I'd had enough of treating his animals, only ever being called in when he had messed around with them so much that the case was hopeless.

'Can I get you anything?' he asked, sounding a little bewildered as I made my way back to the jeep. 'I have the bucket of water ready for you.'

'No thanks. I don't need anything here.'

'But where are you going?' He was beginning to look anxious as I opened the jeep door.

'Well,' I replied, 'as you said, you'd have got the lamb out yourself anyway so there's not much point in your wasting good money on me doing it, is there?'

His face dropped in horror as I moved Slug off the driver's seat to get in. 'Ah, don't be like that, Gillian. Sure, as you're here now, you might as well finish the job off.'

'Not at all. I'll leave it in your capable hands. I'm off to get my dinner.'

'Well, to be honest I'd rather you did it yourself, you know,' he said lamely, trying to avoid eye contact.

'Oh I'm sorry, I must have misunderstood you. I thought you said you could do it yourself.'

With the help of an epidural, I managed to remove the twin lambs through the cervix that Paul had already ripped open. The two lifeless forms were of no use to the ewe as she lay panting miserably in the straw bed. I administered the usual antibiotics and painkillers and left instructions for the next day.

'You could have had two good pedigree lambs there and probably saved the ewe as well if you'd called us earlier,' I reminded Paul as I left the yard, knowing that I was wasting my time.

* * *

My dinner never materialised that evening as I had to go straight back down to the small-animal surgery. A large queue had gathered by the time I arrived, comprising a selection of cats and dogs suffering from a variety of the usual ailments and a trailer with a ewe inside.

I got through the small animals as quickly as I could, but it was still a fair while before I was able to attend to the ewe. From the surgery door I could smell a putrid, rotting lamb. I was suddenly glad that I hadn't made it for dinner.

'Well, Freddie, you can smell this one a mile off.'

At least Freddie was one of our nicer farmers. 'I know, I feel a bit bad about her. I was off spreading fertiliser for the day. I'd only one or two ewes left to lamb and I thought I'd get away with it but it looks like it's too late for this one.'

Freddie was far from being a wealthy farmer but he would never skimp on veterinary attention, no matter how much it ate into his slender pocket. As I looked at the ewe, I knew that he was one of the few that would have brought her in to be treated. She looked like it might be a complete waste of time. My initial reaction was to put her down but, looking at Freddie's concerned face, I decided that if he could make the effort, so could I.

I layered myself with a few gloves before putting a hand into her, knowing the smell would penetrate anyway. My stomach heaved as a trickle of putrid fluid was evacuated by my hand. I shook my head at him as I came up against yet another case of ringwomb. I could only get three fingers inside.

'You're out of luck, Freddie. It's another ringwomb. You've been really plagued with them this year, haven't you?'

'You're not wrong there. I think this is the seventh. Is there any chance you could do a caesarean on her?'

'Not a hope! Those lambs are dead a long time and the infection from her womb would surely kill her.'

With my three fingers, I could just about feel a tiny jaw bone. It came away in my hand as I pulled at it. 'That's how rotten the lambs are.'

The ewe hung her head miserably as I stood up, ready to fill a syringe and put her out of her misery, but Freddie was reluctant. 'She's got this far. Is there nothing at all you can do?'

'Well, I just might be able to remove the lambs in pieces as they're so rotten, but she's had a lot of hardship. Sheep really don't tolerate too much.'

'Don't I know only too well. But can you try?'

The smell was overpowering as I painstakingly extracted the tiny corpses, piece by piece, through the narrow opening. My hands were numb as I carefully pulled out the tiny bones, trying not to tear the ewe's delicate passage. Eventually, I could feel no more and I ran a tube into her womb to irrigate it with an antiseptic solution. Thanks to the epidural injection I had given her at the start, the ewe felt nothing throughout. I injected antibiotics and painkillers but despite my efforts, I didn't hold out much hope for her.

The next morning, having slept with the windows open to try to dilute the noxious vapours, I woke, as usual, to the ringing of the phone.

'Hope I didn't get you out of bed,' said a cocky voice that I instantly recognised.

'Good morning, Paul. What's the problem?'

'Just thought you should know. That ewe died in the night. A good pedigree she was too.'

'Well, if you remember, I told you she would die as you had left her so long before you called us. And, by the way, in future, please call the office number if you have to. My mobile is for emergencies only.' I didn't bother to wait for a reply.

Seconds later it rang again. The ignorance of him, I thought indignantly.

'What's the problem now?' I demanded.

'Oh ... em ... sorry, Gillian. I know it's a bit early to ring you.'

'No, not at all,' I replied, embarrassed as I recognised Freddie's contrite tone. 'What can I do for you?'

'Oh, nothing at all, thanks. You've done enough already. It's just that I thought you'd be interested to know that that ewe is up and looking bright as a button this morning. Cleared her bucket and everything. Thanks again for all your trouble.'

Oh well, I thought to myself. Sometimes it's nice to be wrong.

CHAPTER SIXTEEN

AS SICK AS A DOG

I had always vowed that I would never work with a hangover. This resolution stemmed from a morning 'seeing practice' as a student after a particularly rough night. I had gone down to the practice feeling absolutely fine, though a little bit tired. It was only about two hours later that the hangover really started to kick in. Being driven around in a car over the rough country roads was doing nothing for me and when the vet stopped off at a small shop and returned with two 'thirty percent extra free' bottles of Lucozade, I realised that I must have looked as green as I felt. The Lucozade was quickly soaked up by my parched body and I began to feel a bit more human as we pulled into a well-known racing yard to vet a horse. My job as dogsbody was to trot the horse up and down along the level surface to allow the vet to examine the horse for any signs of lameness. It was only when I started to run along-side the highly-bred animal that I noticed that my legs didn't seem to be in any way connected to my brain. It wasn't until my head hit the hard surface that I realised I had managed to stumble over one of the thoroughbred's hooves. He trotted on gaily without me.

'He must be crooked!' I exclaimed, before dragging myself off the ground. I made my way back to the car without another word and refused to get out of it again until we returned to the practice that evening. If I got slagged by my colleague, his humour was wasted on me as I lay slumped in the passenger seat, vowing never to go to work with a hangover again.

However, despite sticking to this wise resolution, there came the day when I felt worse than I ever had with any hangover and without so much as a drink taken. In college, or while seeing practice, it was quite acceptable to miss the odd day if you were sick and crawl back in under the duvet until the world was a better place. However, when you were part of a busy mixed practice at the height of spring, that just wasn't an option, except in the most extreme cases. The week had started with Seamus having a bad dose of flu. I felt sorry for him when he came into the surgery on the Monday morning, looking worse than any potential patient. The phones kept ringing though, and he slogged on through the day, only heading off to bed after seven that evening, when I offered to cover the night-calls for him. By Wednesday, it was Arthur's turn and he coughed and spluttered but gallantly continued through the day too, treating sick calves and calving cows. By Thursday night, I was back on call again and feeling somewhat proud of myself that I had managed to avoid catching the dose.

I had to admit that I felt a little tired and drained, but that was just from trying to cover the extra workload as Seamus and Arthur, being sick, weren't up to their normal pace. Usually it was I who was the slow one.

Donal poured me a hot whiskey going to bed and I felt quite sure that I would be fine in the morning. But nature had other plans for me.

Three-thirty am saw me heading back down the road in the direction of Jack Duggan's yard: 'An old suckler cow calving with a head stuck out and making no progress,' he informed me in his dour monotone when he rang.

The case was hopeless. The calf was long dead and the only option was to cut up the calf inside the cow to remove it in pieces. Either that or put the cow down, there and then. Jack opted for the former: 'Ye might as well do something useful now that ye'r here,' he told me, as though I had nothing better to be doing at that hour of the night.

It was after five by the time I was back in the jeep, headed for home. Every joint in my body ached with the desperate tiredness that comes with unexpected, unrewarding physical labour at that hour of the night.

I shivered violently despite the car heater being on full blast, while Slug panted all the way home. I crept back into bed with my fleece over my pyjamas, hoping not to wake Donal as I knew he had an early start in the morning. Eventually, I nodded off to sleep, fully enveloped in two thick duvets.

It seemed like only minutes had passed when I was rudely interrupted by the shrill ringing of the alarm clock.

Donal had left for work over an hour before and I hadn't even realised it. I lay there for a while, my body a leaden weight. With great difficulty I got up. My hands shook as I fiddled with my shirt buttons and, despite the heaviest fleece, I still felt frozen to the core. I tried to swallow a few mouthfuls of hot tea but gave up with the sharp, rasping pains that ripped at my throat with every gulp. I added two Panadol to the next mouthful and chucked the remainder down the sink. As I made my way out to the car, a racking cough took over my body and I doubled over, gasping for breath. I had got a few miles down the road before I noticed the pounding in my head and the waves of nausea that washed over me. I pulled in to check the day book. It hadn't even occurred to me to look at it to see where I was supposed to go.

'McDonald's: test 120 cattle (with blood test).' The figures seemed to dance around the page as they mocked me. I started to sweat. My hand trembled as I dialled the office number. Niamh answered after the usual three rings.

'McDonald's. Herd test. Where is it?' I asked her.

'Oh, hi, Gillian!' she answered, not seeming not to notice my unusually abrupt manner. 'He's in Knockabawn. Just go past the cemetery on the left-hand side, up the hill, turn left at the new buildings and he's on the right-hand side, next door to the red cottage.'

It was some time before I realised I was still holding the phone to my ear.

'Are you okay?' asked a voice in the distance. 'You sound a million miles away.'

'I wish I was,' I whispered forlornly as I hung up.

Much and all as I would love to 'ring in sick', there was just too much work to be done by too few vets at that time of year.

In a daze, I made my way to the farm. I stopped off briefly for a bottle of Lucozade but it was no good. My jellied hands couldn't open the seal on the glowing bottle. I resolved again to write to the manufacturers to complain. Why are so many drinks so hard to open just when you need them most?

Jim McDonald, the stockman, seemed a friendly sort as I half-heartedly introduced myself.

'You're very welcome to the area!' he roared, vigorously pumping my frail hand up and down. I was surprised it didn't fall off.

'I hope you're feeling fit this morning,' he continued enthusiastically. 'I'm afraid Kevin that normally works with us is laid up with a bad bout of 'flu.'

I bet he didn't feel as bad as I did; I didn't even have the energy to explain.

'But don't worry,' he continued, 'I've set the crush up well. We won't have any bother getting the cattle through it.'

Where had I heard those words before?

'Which do you want to start with first?' he enquired kindly. 'The cows or the calves?'

He seemed a bit surprised by my subdued answer.

'Whichever will be quieter.'

'I suppose we'll get the cows out of the way first so.' He was beginning to look at me strangely but, in my weakened state, I was past caring.

He was true to his word when he said that he had set up the pens well. Instead of the usual single gate running the cattle into the crush, Jim had ingeniously fixed one gate on top of another. No beast, no matter how highly strung, would manage to scale that barrier. But there was only one problem – it meant that *I* would have to get over it.

As we ran each batch of six cows into the crush, I had to climb in and out over the double barrier. With shaking limbs, I hauled myself up over the swaying obstacle, head spinning, cattle roaring, my targets looming in and out of focus. Despite the physical nature of the work, shivering spasms wracked my body in contrast to the beads of sweat that broke out on my brow. After a while, Jim seemed to sense my reluctance to make conversation. He must have thought I was an unfriendly type.

It seemed to go on forever as I wrote down tag numbers, breed, age and skin measurements, and then carefully clipped and injected each animal. For the first time, a job that had hitherto seemed fairly effortless, now required immense concentration on my part in order to insert the needle into the thick skin and feel for the bleb of tuberculin after each injection. Every female over twelve months of age also had to be blood-tested. After I had made two or three laborious attempts at hauling up the swishing tails, Jim, obviously beginning to wonder at my choice of career, stepped in and wordlessly lifted each tail for me. With a fleeting glimpse of hope, I thought that perhaps I could put off doing the blood tests until the day of the reading, but then realised that I had another large herd test booked in for the Monday when I would have to read this test – I wouldn't have time to do both. There was nothing for it but to carry on.

It seemed to go on forever, but finally the last two cattle ran into the crush, anxious to follow their comrades.

'I'll just run the cows back into the field, but you sit down there. You don't look the best, at all,' said Jim sympathetically and he headed off with his noisy crew of cattle. I slumped down thankfully on a bale of straw.

If I had thought the cows were bad, the calves defeated me altogether – running up and down the crush in twos and threes, bawling, roaring, disappearing out under the bottom bars. I had to stop and hold on to the edges of the crush every now and again to stop my head spinning as I bent over the shaggy creatures. I laboured methodically to inject each calf, with long pauses in between as I waited for each bucking beast to stand still long enough for me to carry out the procedure effectively, knowing full well that I would not have the mental acumen to hit a moving target under the circumstances. The renewed physical exertion brought on fresh bouts of coughing which seemed like they would never end.

Twice, the testing gun fell out of my hand and I stood staring stupidly as it quickly disappeared into the muck. Each time Jim retrieved it, washed it thoroughly and delicately handed it back to me. Rows of figures, noting breed and tag number and skin measurements, merged into a blur. By now, I could no longer summon the energy to help Jim fill the crush: I knew that gate would defeat me. Between each batch, I returned to collapse on my bale and waited until Jim called out to me, 'Ready for you now!'

When we had finished the last batch I didn't even notice and I sat stupidly on my bale, too tired to care.

'I'm sure we could find a few more for you to do if you wanted, but that's all ours done anyway!' Jim joked.

I smiled wanly back at him.

'Come in for a cup of tea. You look like you could use one.'

In the warm kitchen, I eyed the cup of steaming tea cautiously, wondering if the razors in my throat would allow me to swallow it. Mrs McDonald, Jim's elderly mother, tut-tutted in the corner as she eyed me solicitously.

'Lord above, Jim! Can you not see the girl is sick? I always knew veterinary was no job for a woman. Look at the state of her. She's just about worn out. Sure, she's only a scrap of a thing!'

I towered at least a foot and a half over her hunched body but I was too weak to argue.

'Eat up now and get your strength back,' she said setting out a dish of sausages, rashers, eggs and fried bread before me. It was the sort of meal I would usually have devoured with relish but today I just couldn't do it justice. Luckily, Jacko, the little brown and white house dog, had discreetly placed himself under the table beside me and silently took care of most of the sausages and rashers that I smuggled to him from my plate.

Jim saw me off. I tried to hold some sort of a conversation with him as he helped me to carry my blood boxes back to the car.

'Sorry we were a bit slow getting started this morning. Hopefully I'll have thrown off this dose by Monday for the reading. We'll get through them in no time at all.'

'Don't you worry about it. I know it's tough work on a lassie like yourself.'

I cringed inwardly but couldn't dispute the fact that the procedure had taken over an hour longer than normal.

Somehow, I got through the rest of the day and was thankfully able to finish up early.

'Don't even think of going in tomorrow,' Donal warned me when I dragged myself in the door that evening.

That night and the next, I sweated and shivered and ached and coughed, while Slug kept anxious watch over me from my bedside.

We had planned to go out for a meal with some friends on the Saturday night but, instead, ended up sitting by the fire while Donal squeezed bag after bag of oranges and lemons, adding in a generous measure of honey and whiskey each time.

By Monday morning, I was well on the road to recovery but slightly embarrassed about having to face Jim again. Hopefully, I would be able to convince him that I wasn't totally anti-social and that, under normal circumstances, I was quite capable of carrying out my job.

But there was one problem. My day book reminded me: read McDonald's test. But where on earth did they live? I had absolutely no recollection of how I had got there the first day. Hard as I tried, I just couldn't recall any details of the journey. I tried to imagine myself driving around various parts of Wicklow, hoping to jog my memory, but it was useless. In desperation, I rang Donal to see if I had mentioned to him where I had been.

'No, you didn't,' he replied. 'Remember, you weren't able to talk when you got home!'

I had two options: to ring Jim, who already must be thinking that I was a bit dim, or to call the office again. I thought about it for a while and then decided on Jim. I figured that he had already made his mind up that I was useless anyway and that I'd nothing more to lose.

'Hi Jim. Gillian, the vet, here. Just ringing about this morning's reading.' I tried to sound professional.

'Gillian, how are you? No problem at all here – we're all set up for you and Kevin is back in action so you won't have to do any of the heavy work.'

I cringed once more, thinking about how I had slumped helplessly on a bale of hay as Jim had single-handedly herded the cattle into the crush.

'Oh, don't worry, Jim. We could have managed fine on our own. Just one thing though; just remind me where you are again.' I tried to sound casual.

Jim sounded a bit puzzled as he replied. 'We're over at the yard – same place as we tested them. I got the cattle in this morning. We'll have to run them through the crush to read them, won't we?'

'Oh, of course we will, of course,' I laughed, 'but if you could just remind me where the yard is …'

Silence.

'But you were here with us on Friday.'

'Em, yes, that's right, I was.'

Silence.

'So, you know how to get here?'

'Em, no.'

Silence.

'Oh.'

I was beginning to think he had hung up when he began again, slowly and simply explaining as though to a particularly dim child.

'Just go into the village, past the cemetery and ...'

I interrupted him.

'Sorry, Jim. Er ... which village was that again?'

At least, this time around, the reading was done in record time. I was so embarrassed that I kept my head down and the cattle moving as fast as possible through the crush, concentrating with extra diligence on the top and bottom clippings on the side of the necks.

Jim, although courteously friendly, seemed a little bit distant as we made our way through the herd, which, thankfully, was all clear. His conversation was slightly strained. When the job was completed, we headed into the milking parlour for the customary wash and I tried to engage in some light-hearted banter. I left Jim finishing off the clean-up and went back to the jeep.

'Gillian!' he called out after me as I turned on the engine. He thrust a sheet of paper in the window at me. 'You might need this on the way home.'

I had turned out the driveway when I glanced over at the crumpled piece of paper on the passenger seat. I cringed with embarrassment yet again as I recognised the carefully drawn map, beginning at his yard, and detailing exactly how to get back to the office ...

CHAPTER SEVENTEEN

JILL

It was hard to believe that my first spring as a veterinary surgeon was almost over. Despite the adrenalin rush, I could feel the long weeks of late nights and interrupted sleep starting to take its toll on me. Tonight, the evening surgery was quiet and, so far, there were no calls. I decided to make the most of it and head home.

Passing the local takeaway, I was tempted, and I pulled in to order the usual chicken curry for myself, the roast duck with orange for Donal and a bag of the prawn crackers that Slug was so partial to. She crunched contentedly on the passenger seat all the way home.

By the time we got home, Spook and Judy, with their Labrador instinct for food, were waiting patiently for us, and they stared with rapt concentration at the brown paper bag as though willing it to open.

'Sorry, Judy, you know what happened last time,' I said, pushing the three sorrowful-looking dogs out the door and closing it firmly behind them. Despite her breeding,

Judy had a sensitive stomach and I had already discovered that it didn't mix well with chicken curry.

Deciding to be civilised, we opened a bottle of wine with the meal and I was feeling slightly more human as I ran a hot bath. By ten o'clock I was in bed, enjoying a rare early night. I picked up a book that I'd started reading over three months previously and lazily flicked through a few pages. Without noticing, I passed from wakefulness to sleep. I was back at a college reunion, in the local from our student days. We were all busy discussing our new jobs until, suddenly, the barman turned into the dean. He told us that we all had to re-sit our Leaving Certificate exams as it had come to light that we had never passed it in the first place; maths – paper one, was at nine o'clock the next morning. I was in a panic because I knew that I had to read a herd test at the same time. I was trying to ring Donal to ask him if he would read the test for me when the phone rang. I pulled it out of my pocket and knocked the off button but still it rang. It rang four or five times, until, with a start, I awoke from my dream. I looked in surprise to see Donal lying in the bed beside me and then saw the flashing light on the phone.

The anxious voice on the other end of the phone quickly brought me back to reality with a jolt.

'It's Kevin Ryan here. I'm really sorry to ring you at this hour but I'm a bit worried about Jill. She's been off form for the last few days and she won't get out of her bed now. It's not at all like her.'

Jill was the farm collie and I had often admired her, though only from a distance. She was a typical working dog and lived only for her job. She had no interest in the usual comforts of life or in the silly antics of the other yard dogs; remaining aloof from them, she waited only for the command to work. Although I had often seen her slinking around in the distance or disappearing at speed after some rebel sheep, until now, I had never come into close contact with her. My presence was of absolutely no interest to her and I always felt that she was somewhat dismissive of Slug, refusing to join in any of the frenzied barking matches that usually accompanied my arrival.

Kevin had first expressed his concerns to me a few weeks previously as I'd struggled to deliver an oversized calf from a nervous and resentful heifer. Jill was ten years old and had never had pups. But during her last heat, she had escaped for a few minutes one day and, six weeks later, the telltale signs of pregnancy were all too obvious. Tonight, it seemed that Kevin's fears were justified. According to him, she was now four days overdue, a delay which was very significant in dog terms. Apparently, they had tried to leave her in the yard to rest as her time approached but, in her desperation to get on with her job and the life that she knew, she had managed to scale a high wall and escape.

The first the Ryans knew of it was when a shaggy form came hurtling across the fields towards them, although they had had a fifteen-minute drive to the out-farm. Because Jill was so determined, they had decided she would be happier working and so she had spent a blissful day doing what she knew best. Although she seemed tired that evening, she was equally determined to join in again on the two following days and reluctantly they allowed her, fearing the worst if they left her behind. Now, at the end of the third day, Jill had returned and then collapsed in a corner of the shed.

I lay back on the warm pillows and closed my eyes for just a couple of moments before hauling myself out and throwing on some clothes. There is an art with night calls which, with practice, allows you to time perfectly the moment at which you come out of automatic pilot mode and actually wake up. When perfected, it allows you to dress and drive to the call while still feeling like you are actually in bed.

'Will you be long?' muttered Donal drowsily as I dressed.

'Not sure,' I replied. 'Maybe not.' It doesn't take long to put a dog to sleep.

Slug eyed me balefully as I picked up the car keys and with a martyred look made her way down the stairs. Spook and Judy awoke from where they slumbered in front of the warm stove. They gallantly escorted us to the door, nails clicking on the tiled floor, but weren't in any way anxious to join us. When I opened the jeep door for Slug, instead of jumping in as she usually does, she just stood there. Obviously she was good at automatic pilot mode too. I picked her up and deposited her on the passenger seat where she slumped into a ball and never stirred for the rest of the journey.

I was very worried. Dogs like Jill can be incredibly difficult to treat because they often refuse to acknowledge pain. It is not unknown for a tough collie to work the day out on a broken leg and only show signs of lameness when the job is finished. If Jill had collapsed, something was very seriously amiss.

Despite my best efforts to stay asleep, my mind buzzed as I drove the thirty miles to the surgery where I had arranged to meet Kevin. There was no point in going directly to the farm as I was sure that Jill would need drastic treatment if she was to pull through this crisis. Minutes of delay could prove fatal.

Kevin was waiting for me when I got there. I was shocked to see Jill lying collapsed in a bundle. The towel in which she was wrapped was stained with a mixture of fresh and clotted blood. When I probed deep in her tense abdomen, shrill yelps interrupted her gasping breath. I shuddered when I saw the ghostly white of the mucous membranes in her mouth. Jill was clearly dying.

I shook my head sadly at Kevin. 'I'm sorry, but she's in big trouble. I think she should have had those pups a couple of days ago. Something's gone drastically wrong.'

I could barely hear him as he whispered, 'Is there nothing at all we can do?'

I hesitated. My initial reaction was to put Jill to sleep but I was repulsed by the thought of being responsible for the demise of such a wonderful dog.

'I could try opening her up to see exactly what has happened, but I doubt she'd survive the anaesthetic.'

'Please try anyway, Gillian!' he begged.

I ushered Kevin out the door with no more assurance than, 'I'll let you know – either way.'

I checked my watch: it was ten past one. I was suddenly

acutely aware of my limited surgical skills but at this hour of night I was reluctant to ring for help, especially as I knew that Seamus had worked through until after four the previous morning, while Arthur was off on a week's leave. The necessity for speed didn't allow me to think as I set up the warm intravenous drip, infused with steroids to counteract the shock. Somewhere in the back of my mind, I worried about the potential side-effects such as gastric ulceration, delayed tissue healing and increased risk of infection, but I dismissed them just as quickly as I felt that Jill was too far gone to worry about such things.

Cautiously, I administered half the calculated dose of anaesthetic and thanked God for my habit, born of inexperience, of always under-dosing through lack of confidence; within seconds Jill was deeply anaesthetised – any more and the night's work would have been over.

Having clipped and prepped my sleeping patient, I stood, with scalpel in hand, poised over her still form draped in surgical green. I rapidly incised the thin skin and the fibrous muscle midline. A stream of curses erupted to match the gush of putrid, green-black fluid that sprayed from my neat incision. I was sure I hadn't incised the uterus and yet how else could I have released all this fluid? I tried to reassure myself that the dog would have died anyway and it wasn't purely due to my incompetence, as I enlarged the opening and eased out the rotting womb.

With a surge of mixed relief and shock, I noticed a large tear in the cranial horn that couldn't possibly have been caused by my scalpel. The shrivelled edges indicated that it had been torn for some time, thus explaining the large blood clots. I glanced anxiously at Jill's chest and was relieved to notice a faint yet perceptible movement. As I groped the stodgy mass, I could feel several afterbirths and one lifeless pup swilling around in the ruptured uterus. There had to be more than one.

As I tried to extract the mass from the abdomen I could feel something hard, just out of reach, under the loops of intestine. Quickly, I fished out another pup. With increasing disbelief, I recovered two more – one from deep down beside the bladder and one tucked neatly under the liver. No textbook could ever have prepared me for this freakish occurrence. I wondered just how long these pups had been floating around, suffocated in their own fluid, as Jill continued to work. I felt a twinge of pity for the four lifeless forms lying on the stainless steel tray among the debris of afterbirths and placental fluid but, right now, my thoughts were more for Jill.

I couldn't believe that any animal could survive so much. Should I call a halt now? And yet, we had come this far and it seemed a shame not to give her a chance.

I swabbed out as much of the mucky fluid as I could, in order to allow me to see what I was operating on. By now the floor was littered with dozens of soiled swabs as the clinical waste bucket was literally overflowing. It didn't worry me that I hadn't obtained Kevin's permission to remove Jill's womb beforehand: I was quite sure that under the circumstances he would understand.

The stretched ligament of the heavily pregnant uterus made it easy to pull up the ovaries and ligate them. When it came to tying off the neck of the womb, I laughed grimly to myself, thinking of the tidy diagrams of fancy suture patterns that we had so painstakingly learnt in college, for situations less dire than this. I did my best to imitate the picture as I worked on the rotting tissue and wasn't surprised when it just didn't look the same. With dismay I examined the remaining contents of the abdomen, awash with rotted tissue fragments bathed in the green-black fluid.

By now, my back ached with tension and it seemed a long time since I had been asleep in bed. I thought with envy of the veterinary programmes on TV, where a fresh team of surgeons, aided by a horde of trained nurses, would take over at this stage. I shivered as the coldness that comes only with exhaustion penetrated deep into my bones. Tonight, it was only myself and Slug, sitting patiently at my feet, wrinkling her nose slightly when the smell got too much even for her.

By the time I had flushed four litres of warmed fluids through the abdomen, it was starting to look a bit healthier and, taking a last reluctant look, I began the final stitch-up. Jill's shallow and irregular breathing penetrated my consciousness as I wearily placed the last few sutures.

I seemed to be working in slow motion as I dried as much of her soaked coat as possible. I then wrapped her up in some heavy blankets and propped her up with a row of hot water bottles in the heated kennel. I suspended the remainder of her drip from the hook that served as a drip stand. The rest was up to Jill.

I roughly hosed down the worst of the mess and decided to leave the final clean-up until the next morning, too tired to worry about incurring Niamh's wrath. It was by now after two o'clock, and I was surprised when Kevin answered the phone on the first ring. I explained as briefly as I could and told him that, although Jill had come this far, I still didn't think that she could possibly make it. His voice was subdued as he thanked me for trying.

It was almost three o'clock in the morning by the time I got home for the second time that day. Spook and Judy were eagerly waiting at the door, having heard the approaching car. After a quick sniff, Slug jumped up on to the recently vacated couch, worn out by the day's events.

Wearily, I gave Donal a brief outline of what had happened.

'Sounds like a nightmare. Will she live?' he asked.

'I don't know. I just don't know,' I replied gloomily.

I tossed and turned in the bed, trying to relieve my aching back. I slept fitfully, interrupted by nightmarish scenes of drowning pups and dying dogs.

By six o'clock, I could bear it no longer and I got up, not bothering to shower, and drove back to the surgery. I unlocked the door and felt sick thinking of the sight of the dead dog that might await me.

I stared in disbelief as I looked at a thin, but alert, figure sitting upright in her kennel, still attached to the drip, glancing upwards occasionally with interest at the cat who was boarded on the top row. With growing amazement, I checked over the docile patient. Temperature, normal; colour, still pale but with a decidedly pinkish hue; abdomen, no pain or tenseness; wound, looking good.

Over the next few days, Jill improved with a speed that I

didn't think possible. Soon she was home with her delighted owner. I felt overjoyed that, finally, I had, without doubt, saved the life of an animal. So many days are spent administering treatments and wondering what, if any, real effect they will have on the final outcome. On that day, I basked in the knowledge that, without me, Jill would most certainly have died.

I didn't see Jill for quite some time as Kevin's farm went through a relatively peaceful spell. Jill, in typical collie form, pulled her own stitches out. It must have been six months later when I pulled into the yard to 'wash out' a few cows. I laughed to myself, reflecting that if I hadn't been able to get near Jill on my previous visits, I certainly wouldn't get near her now. In her mind, I would be the one who had taken her from her rightful job, confined her in a kennel and carried out numerous unpleasant procedures on her. Still, I hoped to catch a glimpse of her – just to prove to my disbelieving mind that all was still well.

As I opened the car door, I was taken aback as a black and white form shot across the yard, straight to the car and deposited itself on my lap. I stared in disbelief at Jill. She in turn sat gazing devotedly at me, totally ignoring poor Slug who was quite put out by this rude invasion.

To this day, any time I go into that yard Jill repeats the performance and I can do nothing without having a gentle nose glued to my wellington boot. In fact, sometimes, on those bad days when everything I look at seems to die, I drive by Jill's farm just to reassure myself that at least one animal in the whole of Wicklow really appreciates me.

CHAPTER EIGHTEEN

THE BACHELOR PAD

I remember once, as a student, being let out on a call on a busy spring evening to treat a cow with redwater. The farmers lived in a high-density tick area and they had observed the classic red urine caused by the tick-borne parasite which breaks down the cow's red blood cells. The diagnosis was obvious over the phone and the treatment straightforward enough for me to administer even with my limited skills as a student. Nevertheless, I was walking on air as I made my way up to the small hill farm. Until now, I had always accompanied the vet but this time it was just me. However, despite managing to do the job efficiently, I thought, the two farmers eyed me suspiciously in stony silence for the duration of my visit and apparently I had no sooner left the yard than they were on the phone to the office to see what time the real vet was coming out.

It was the same eerie silence that reminded me of that day now. Although more than three years later and with a good six months of experience under my belt, it seemed that nothing had changed.

When I finally qualified, I was pleasantly surprised that the local farmers, unaccustomed and all as they were to having a real live female vet, seemed to warm quickly to the idea. After a couple of calls, they even dropped the 'lady vit' title and I became just an ordinary 'vit'. But up in the mountainy highlands, in sparse patches where the hills rose above the clouds, it seemed that the revolution had never caught on.

'Ballinacarraig, TB-test thirty sucklers': it had seemed an innocent enough entry in the day-book that morning.

I was lost in another world as I headed up over the mountain, enjoying the tranquillity of the morning. The directions Niamh had given me that morning had guided me to a tiny, almost derelict cottage, tucked into the edge of a steep bank. Looking at it, I found it hard to believe that the three elderly brothers who owned the farm and had been born and reared there still lived in such conditions. As though from another era, the brothers were almost totally self-sufficient and only ventured down to the bright lights of Wicklow town once a month for essential supplies. While driving up the ever-narrowing roadway, I had noticed that the electricity and telephone wires had long since run out and, not for the first time, it amazed me to find people living no more than thirty miles from Dublin without such basic supplies.

My cogitations were cut short as I pulled into the yard. Up on the hill, I observed three bearded men, dressed in identical soiled overcoats and worn boots. They appeared to be quietly contemplating me from the makeshift cattle crush where the herd of sucklers was penned.

Opening the door of the jeep, I called out a greeting, but was a bit taken aback as the three men stared into the distance, seemingly oblivious to my very presence.

Oh well, I thought to myself, in and out, get it over with.

Loaded down with the familiar McClintock TB testing syringes hanging in my belt and the usual array of blood bottles, note-book, pen, scissors and the well-worn callipers, I headed up the hill. As I neared my clients, although by now slightly out of breath, I renewed my greeting. I began to feel a little bit unnerved when there was still no reply. Their silence was in stark contrast to the frenzied yelping of the farm collie as he snapped deliriously around my heels, and the constant roars and bawls of the corralled cows and calves.

'Right, are we ready so?' I tried again, mustering up as much enthusiasm as I could.

There was a long pause as the three shuffled uncomfortably, eyes cast to the ground.

Eventually, the middle man looked up out over my shoulder and with the half of the mouth that wasn't supporting his pipe, growled out:

'Where's the vit?'

'Oh, I'm sorry,' I replied cheerfully. 'I'm new to the practice. I should have introduced myself! My name is Gillian and I've come to test the cattle.'

I thrust my hand forward to the spokesman but quickly withdrew it as I realised the only likely contact would be from the snapping teeth of the dog as he hurled himself

ceaselessly up and down by my side. In hindsight, I realised that he too may have been upset by the rare sighting
of the female of the species and trying to protect his terri-
tory from the unfamiliar invasion.

'Well now, thim's big cattle and I think the boss man
should come up himself. 'Tisn't a job for a wan like yer-
self.'

His two siblings mutely assented with an almost imperceptible nod of the head.

The time for patience was over. I planned on spending
as little time as possible here, and standing around discussing the merits of the boss was not the way forward.

'Not at all!' I cried happily. 'We'll manage grand. Now, if
you could just start running the cattle into the crush, we'll
be done in no time.'

Loading the avian and bovine tuberculins into the
respective syringes, I strode off towards the top of the
crush and whipped out my notebook, ready for action,
while all the time aware of the silence behind me.

Turning back, I noticed the three men still standing
where I left them as though immobilised by fear of this
unknown entity.

Desperate measures were clearly called for, so, carefully
packing the syringes back into the belt, I hopped over the
fence into the holding pen and began to herd the bewildered animals into the crush.

My action worked perfectly, as Mr Spokesman immediately followed me, flanked on either side by his comrades,
with a speed I would never have suspected them capable
of, as though they were anxious to protect the cattle from

me. Satisfied, I hopped back out and began silently noting down breeds, sexes and tag numbers.

It wasn't going to be as bad as I thought, I decided a while later, observing the rapidly dwindling number of cattle in the pen. Three more crush-loads and I would be on my way. Casually, I hummed to myself to lighten the ordeal, but hastily stopped when I observed the shocked expression on the wizened faces of my clients.

Before I knew it, the last three cattle were in the crush but, just as I was reloading the syringe full of tuberculin, the inevitable happened. The most skittish of the group, a wiry black whitehead, decided that enough was enough and suddenly plunged her way through the rotted planks of the makeshift pen. The splintering of wood alerted me just in time to see her bucking her way up the hill to rejoin her comrades with a triumphant bellow.

Why today? I thought to myself wearily, as I threw down my scissors and notepad to race back up the hill after the escapee. I turned briefly to see which way the men had headed to block the great escape and looked in bewilderment, realising that they hadn't even budged from where they were standing.

'Quick!' I roared. 'We'll have to catch her before she gets out on the hill!'

Still they stood and stared.

With a frustrated glance at the fast-disappearing beast, I stopped. 'We'll have to get her back. She has to be tested on the same day as all the others.'

'Ye won't catch her today,' was the grim response as they continued to gaze vacantly at the far horizon, now rapidly being approached by the fleeing Charolais.

'Well, we'll have to. It's the Department's rules, not mine,' I said firmly, hoping that the reference to the payers of subsidies would help me out.

'Ye won't catch her today,' the most talkative of the trio repeated as though reciting a mantra.

Hopelessly, I threw myself back on the remains of the crush, head spinning with the prospect of a day of irate clients, for whom I would now be considerably late.

On days like these, how I would love to call out the powers-that-be and enlist them in the battle to retrieve this one stubborn cow from the hilltops. Little would they know how one single entry in the testing book of skin measurements before and three days after the tuberculin injection could cause me such grief. What difference was this one escapee going to make to the health records of the national herd? As my conscience battled with my sanity, I raised my head and saw that the three, oblivious to my anguish, had begun the slow descent down the hill towards the ruin that served as their dwelling place. That decided me.

'Come back!' I roared after them, the first raised voice of the day. 'She has to be done even if it means putting the whole lot of them through again!'

'She won't be caught in a hurry,' came the gruff reply.

'Well then,' I said firmly, 'I'll wait until she is.'

The brothers paused and glared at me in unison as though wondering from what planet I had descended. Then, wordlessly, they made their way back up the steep incline. As I laid down my testing belt and made to follow, the spokesman half-turned and with a dismissive glance at me, growled, 'Don't ye follow, ye'll only drive them wild!'

Fine so, I thought to myself, impervious to insult at this stage, as I slumped down on the nearest log. Eventually, I heard the roar of distant cattle, accompanied by the shrill yelping of the dog.

Relieved, I watched as they made steady progress down the hill, but just as they came over the hollow which would lead them back into the holding pen, the original culprit turned tail and broke rank, quickly to be followed by her increasingly nervous comrades. Silently cursing, I sank back on the log and watched the three again make their way back up the steep slopes with slow, even steps.

Apart from the time that was being eaten out of my already busy day, the delay was beginning to cause me another increasingly urgent problem. Since before I had got out of the car, I had needed to go to the toilet. Initially, I had ignored the problem, but as time ticked by, the need was becoming more and more pressing.

Of all the problems encountered by a female vet, this is one that can occasionally result in rather embarrassing situations. Despite the odd nudge and wink among the menfolk, nothing is thought of a male vet stepping into a dim corner of a dusty hay shed after a particularly long calving or long-drawn-out test. For the lady vet, however, it would be unthinkable, although on a few occasions one becomes desperate enough to attempt it. More than once, I have sent a surprised farmer off for a fresh bucket of water when there was already a perfectly good one on hand. One gentleman farmer whom I had to attend on a regular basis, seemed to have an intuitive understanding of the delicacy of the problem and on every occasion before I began the job would discreetly ask if I 'would care to use the facilities'.

However, judging from my experience so far, I wasn't holding out for any such consideration from today's clients. Carefully throwing a glance around to pick out a suitable bush, I gave up all hope as the nearest solid item to the holding pen was the house itself. My only chance was to perform in the stark openness of the barren field and hope I didn't cause heart failure if any of the three farmers should choose the wrong moment to reappear. Just I was beginning to plan my route, the sound of the approaching cattle put paid to my plans and I braced myself for another wait.

This time, the cattle broke in the opposite direction and headed down towards the house. The unfamiliar surroundings caused them to split and, with increasing frenzy, they careered around the rough slopes. Pulling myself together, I got up and started towards the end of the field, ignoring the cold stares of my fellow herdsmen. While I waved and roared at the bewildered cattle, they took one look at me and stampeded past the pen. Luckily, and by what seemed like divine intervention, half of them managed to run into it, so panic-stricken were they in their attempt to escape from me. Gleefully, I observed that my victim had managed to wedge herself between the stock bull and a particularly large cow. Seizing my moment, and regardless of the stares of the men and the indignant yelping which followed close on my heels, I leapt up on to the last remaining plank and, with lightning speed, clipped and injected the animal. I barely had time to jump down again before, with a sharp crack, the entire fence gave way. Luckily, I just managed to fall clear of the rail before it caught over the back of the enraged bull who proceeded to carry his harness at speed in the direction of the distant horizon.

'Right so,' I said as casually as I dared, while the men surveyed the ruins before them, 'we're all done.'

But as the adrenalin of my success faded, I realised that after my acrobatics, I wasn't going to make it out of the place intact. Obviously, the jumping around had stretched my bladder wall so that now the pain was excruciating as I slowly walked cross-legged down the field. A sweat had begun to break out on my forehead by the time I made up my mind.

'Sorry,' I began hesitantly, in the general direction of my clients, 'but could I use your toilet, please?'

If I thought the silence before was bad, I wasn't prepared myself for what was to come. The three stopped as though frozen in their tracks and stared long and hard at me. Then the spokesman finally stepped forward and beckoned with a nod of his head for me to follow him, leaving the other two behind. My agony overcame my embarrassment as I followed meekly into the ancient dwelling with its bare stone floor, sparsely furnished with three chairs, a small table and a gas ring. Glancing around, I wondered where the toilet was and was about to follow my host through the low door into the only adjoining room when he reappeared. In the dim light, I could barely make out the rusted bucket which he unceremoniously dumped on the floor in front of me. He then disappeared back out the front door, firmly closing the latch. Such was my relief, that it might well have been the main toilet in the White House. As the pains began to subside, I cautiously straightened myself up again and, carefully picking up the bucket, glanced over at the filthy enamelled sink which stood in the corner, packed with dishes from the morning's breakfast. No tap filled into the sink and the only exit was out an old rubber pipe which drained through the thick walls. Trying to move as noiselessly as possible, I took out all the dirty dishes before sloshing the voluminous quantities of straw-coloured liquid into the sink. Spying a similar bucket underneath, which after a quick smell I ascertained to be water, I poured a quantity down after my sample before reloading the dishes.

The three men were huddled by the battered old Fiat which represented their only contact with the outside world. They barely raised their eyes as I cheerfully informed them that I would see them again in three days' time. My feeling of relief gradually gave way to growing embarrassment as their stony stares seemed to bore into me. Thankfully, I threw my gear into the back of the boot and without even stopping to pull off my overalls, I jumped into the car and slammed the door. As I turned the key, I slammed my foot down on the accelerator, such was my haste to get away as quickly as possible. Before I realised what had happened, the jeep came to a sudden halt and the silence was filled with the raw sound of crunching metal and shattered glass. In horror, I looked down at the gear-stick to see it firmly placed in reverse.

Stepping out of the car apprehensively, I made my way to the rear. My tow-bar lay wedged deep into the middle of the Fiat's ancient bumper. The ground was strewn with the debris of the only remaining light unit on the car. The only perceptible change in the faces of the men was a slight paling of the weathered skin, subtly visible beneath their unkempt beards. I braced myself for the volley of abuse which, under any normal circumstances, would have followed, but instead was greeted with deathly silence as the three huddled wordlessly over the vehicle, examining the dent in the crumpled metal.

I'd had enough for one day. Proffering a muttered apology, to which there was no reply, I assured the trio that I would fix up with them on my return visit in three days' time. I then got back into the jeep and, forcing the gear-stick into first gear, slowly pulled off, wincing slightly at the screech as the tow-bar became disengaged from the rusted metal.

My last view of my clients was in the rear view mirror. The three sets of eyes followed my hasty retreat with haunted expressions, while their dog pursued my car as though baying for my blood.

CHAPTER NINETEEN

FOND FAREWELL

My patient was an elderly Labrador, a quiet, dignified type, despite the bandy hind legs and the emaciated frame. Meg had become an old favourite of mine as I had treated her over the past few months for her numerous geriatric ailments. Her arthritic left hip, her failing heart and worn-out kidneys, meant that I had come to be well acquainted with not only Meg, but also the elderly couple who owned her. No matter what I did, Meg responded only with a sheepish look and a wagging tail. It was clear that both she and her owners had absolute faith in me – little aid with which to fight the ravages of old age.

I tried not to think of my own Judy, whose temperament and geriatric ailments seemed to mirror exactly those of the dog now being gently hoisted on to the consulting table.

'Well,' said Mr Doyle, 'what do you think of our lassie this time?'

I could sense the pain behind the forced gaiety in his voice. Mrs Doyle was unusually silent, fiddling nervously with the strap of her bag. I ran my hands gently over the aged body and I was aware of trusting brown eyes gazing expectantly at me.

Meg knew.

As I listened intently to the muffled heartbeat, silent memories came unbidden to my mind: a vigorous, glossy-coated animal, galloping freely across the far hill, absorbed in the excitement of a rough-and-tumble game of tag. An otter-like head breaking the water, effortlessly propelled by invisible legs. A frenzied roll in the long grass, head ecstatically thrashing from side to side. I forced myself to put the memories from my mind.

Carefully, I manipulated Meg's left hip, cringing at the rough grating of bone on bone. She grinned apologetically but I couldn't help noticing how her body seemed to sag with the weight of the chronic pain that she was now experiencing, despite the best available therapy.

Mrs Doyle's hand seemed frail as she gently stroked the silken ears. Placing the stethoscope over the dog's bony chest, I listened to the all too familiar swooshing of her leaky valves and the congested chest that even the best medication had failed to alleviate. As though to confirm my findings, she coughed deeply and the scent of failing kidneys was heavy on her breath.

I tried to expel the images of a black and yellow ball, lying snugly in a deep bed of sweet-smelling straw, as my Judy lay, exhausted after the day's exertions, her golden coat in stark contrast to that of Spook's glossy black.

With a discreet nod, I signalled to Niamh to leave. Barely trusting myself to speak, I took my client's hand and for the first time, raised my eyes to hers.

'Mrs Doyle, I think the time has come.'

There was no need for lengthy explanations. We all knew that we were just putting off the inevitable day with the battery of medications that had become a part of the daily routine. We had discussed on many occasions how when the time would come, Meg would be spared the indignity of a slow and painful death. The Doyles knew in their hearts that their beloved dog's race was run. All they needed was my confirmation.

Not wanting to prolong the heartbreak, I briskly filled the syringe, blinking the tears out of my eyes. My hand shook slightly as I inserted the needle into the fragile vein. Meg's tail thumped out a soft rhythm on the steel table. It echoed a rhythm in my mind. As I depressed the plunger, the tail gradually slowed and the rhythm faded as her frail body slumped in Mrs Doyle's arms.

At peace.

I gulped deeply, trying to dispel the haunting images of a cold body, set in the rigid pose of death. But I could not hold back the tears as I shook the trembling hands of Mr and Mrs Doyle in turn and whispered an inadequate 'I'm sorry.' I admired the strength of the elderly man and woman as they thanked me in faltering voices for my care. Mrs Doyle took one look back and, placing her hand in mine, whispered in my ear, 'Thank you for sharing our tears.'

When the door had shut, I could no longer control the

flood. A torrent of tears streamed down my face as I looked down at the lifeless form on the table. I felt slightly guilty that, although I shared the pain of the old couple for the loss of their dog, my tears were being shed for my own beloved Judy, who had undergone a similar fate only two days previously.

Judy had come to me some years earlier. I had travelled to Kildare to buy a Labrador pup advertised in the local papers but, when I got there, ended up feeling sorry for the bitch instead, due to the cramped conditions in which she was kept. The owner seemed slightly surprised, but was happy to part with her for cash. The day I bought her, I took her up to the fields behind where we lived and despite her long confinement in a small dog enclosure, she had run and run and run, in ever widening circles around me, as though her life depended on it. When the last of her energy was spent, she came back to my heel and never took her eyes off me as we walked slowly home.

Spook had arrived a few months later and, from the day I drove home with the two of them together in the back of an ancient Renault 4, they became best buddies. If you saw one, the other was never far behind. Judy was the sensible one while Spook, at only six months of age, was always getting into scrapes. Before Spook's arrival, Judy had always accompanied me in the car, but now having two large Labradors in the tiny vehicle was a bit of a tight squeeze. One day, I left them parked outside a local shop to run in for a pint of milk. While Judy snuggled peacefully on the passenger seat, Spook somehow managed, in her exuberance, to knock off the hand-brake. I came out to find my little blue Renault a good six feet from where I had left it and with a nice big dent in the bumper. Thankfully, it had run into a lamp-post and not another car.

But once they were together, Spook and Judy didn't care what they did. Left at home, they would happily potter around the garden or snooze in front of the fire until I returned. They often accompanied Donal and myself on our walks in the early days, and so they settled in quickly to their new home when we got married. So good-natured were they that they didn't seem to mind the addition of Slug in the least and weren't at all put out when she usurped them as the car dog. When out on walks the three would play together happily enough, but back home Slug became aloof and so the two Labs became even more of a twosome.

As time went by, Judy, worn down by years of breeding, and with naturally bad hips, slowed down a lot and Spook, with growing maturity, seemed to slow with her – at least most of the time. I became accustomed to the continuous clicking of Judy's left hip as she bunny-hopped alongside us.

But things can't stay the same forever and the day I had to carry Judy from where she had collapsed on the front step, with Spook sitting loyally beside her, my mind was made up.

As I looked for the last time into those ever-trusting brown eyes, Spook sat motionless for the first time in her life, as though sensing the gravity of the moment.

When all was done, Donal and I took Spook up to the forest where the three of us walked for hours, retracing the many, many steps that we had taken as a foursome over the previous years. And when we returned, even Slug seemed strangely subdued.

The next day, I left Slug at home with Spook for company but returned to find Spook lying cold and miserable with an old teddy bear that had belonged Judy.

On the Monday, I took the two to work with me but Spook lay on the passenger floor and even when we got to a friendly farm where I knew she would be welcome, I had to pull her out by the collar.

That night, I woke for a glass of water, and went downstairs to find Spook lying on the floor and Slug beside her, methodically licking the silken coat – a gesture which I had never seen before.

Up to now, Spook had always had a typical Labrador appetite but now she barely picked at the piece of freshly roasted chicken I gave her.

I had often offered advice to clients in relation to a grieving pet and now I frantically tried to recall my words of wisdom. Lots of exercise, distraction, TLC – Spook just wasn't interested. I was off duty the following Sunday, so we packed the boot and loaded Slug and the downcast Spook into the back seat and headed for Greystones beach – always a favourite for Spook, who was a strong swimmer.

The fresh sea air and the brightness of the day should have cheered us all up but it just reminded me of the last time we had been there only a few short weeks before. Slug had stayed at home, being contemptuous of water. Judy loved the freedom of swimming, while Spook, as usual, swam straight out to sea, as though heading for Wales. We occupied ourselves throwing stones for Judy and laughed as she duck-dived into the shallow surf in a most undoglike fashion. After a few throws, I looked back for Spook, only to realise with alarm that she was by now some distance out.

'Spook!' I yelled, making Judy jump. The little head bobbed happily on the waves, totally ignoring me.

'Come in, Spook!' I gestured, my right hand high in the air. It was most unlike her to ignore me and I began to panic. I ran alongside the shore until I was almost level with her. She was swimming at an angle, gradually getting closer, but still she ignored me.

'Spook,' I roared, and as I did so, I noticed not one, but two dogs close on my heels – there were Judy and Spook, frisking along behind me. I looked again in astonishment at the dog in the water, only to realise that the little black head in the water was not a dog at all but a seal!

'Some vet you are!' laughed Donal.

As the seal came closer, the dogs noticed him too and Judy set up a frantic barking which the seal utterly ignored.

A few times Spook made to swim out to him but each time, she lost her nerve. She'd get about halfway out, and then think better of it and surf the waves back to me with powerful strokes as though afraid of being chased.

But today, she wouldn't even go into the water, trailing miserably along behind me. And by the following week, I was getting really worried as she was now losing weight despite my best efforts at hand-feeding her.

Seamus laughed initially when I asked him to have a look at her for me, but then quickly agreed when he saw I was serious.

'You know yourself there's nothing physically wrong with her,' he said as he finished the most detailed clinical examination I had yet seen him carry out on any animal.

Between us, we decided to start her on some anti-anxiety medication; but, if anything, it made her mope even more. By now, I was bringing her everywhere with me, and Slug loyally sat on the back seat beside her, abandoning her usual front-seat perch.

On the following Friday, I had to carry Spook in the surgery door to the evening clinic, Slug following behind.

'Ah, the poor dog,' commented a well-meaning client as she held the door open for me. 'Is she very old?'

Spook was only six.

I muttered a reply and brought Spook out the back. The once glossy coat was now dull and listless. With a shock, I noticed the greying muzzle as though seeing it for the first time. Her eyes, once bright and vibrant, lay sunken in her head and I noticed a slight yellowish hue to her membranes. As I stroked the familiar body, I was appalled at the ribs that not long ago had been well-padded. I pulled the silken ears through my fingers and she didn't even lift her head in response.

The door opened and Seamus walked in. 'There's two or three out there waiting …' he began, then cut off when he saw my face. 'Don't worry, I'll look after them,' he said, and closed the door behind him.

Only three short weeks after Judy had been put to sleep, Spook followed her. As always in life, where one went the other was never far behind.

CHAPTER TWENTY

A JOB WELL DONE

Another two miles and I would be home. I was on call for the night but as we were into summer, the quiet time of year, I wasn't expecting much trouble. In my mind I had already reached my destination and was sharing a bottle of wine with Donal in front of the fire when the shrill ringing of the phone shattered my illusion.

'Hello there. Gerry O'Donnell speaking. I don't think we've met before.'

He sounded like an affable enough sort of person – definitely not like the usual late-night troublemaker that decides at ten o'clock at night that the sick calf (the one which they didn't think justified a call-out for the last three days) suddenly does – urgently.

'What can I do for you?' I inquired politely.

'Well, I'm sorry to disturb you at this hour and it's probably nothing, but I don't want to leave it go and then have to get you out of bed later. I've a Limousin cow here that's due to calve and she's been off on her own for the best part of the day but nothing much is happening. She's not forcing or showing any signs of getting on with the job. I wonder would it would be safe enough to leave her?'

'Well, it's hard to say without examining her. Has she put out a water bag at all?'

'She did around lunchtime. That's why I was expecting a bit of progress by now.'

I got a sudden sinking feeling in my stomach. I tend to have an over-vivid imagination, especially late at night, but this cow sounded like she could possibly have a twisted uterus and I'd never dealt with one on my own before. Even at the best of times, I knew it wasn't an easy job.

'Sure, she'll probably come to no harm before morning, will she?' Gerry interrupted. 'I don't like dragging you all the way out at this hour.'

It was so tempting to agree with him and forget about the cow for the night, but my imagination had gone into overdrive and I was already visualising the twisted uterus filling up with fluid, making a bad situation worse.

'No, I think you're right to be worried. If you could get her into the shed, please, I'll be down to you in about half an hour.'

'Well, if you're sure it's not too much trouble. She's a good pedigree cow, right enough.'

His words didn't exactly console me but the sooner I got there, the sooner I would know.

Reluctantly, I turned the jeep around and continued back down the road I had just driven up. Before I knew it I had reached the yard, following Gerry's clear instructions – another first for a Wicklow farmer.

'You made it in right good time,' said Gerry warmly. 'I hope I haven't put you to a wasted journey.'

The Limousin cow eyed me suspiciously as she stood in her stall, carelessly pulling at the odd wisp of hay. Certainly she didn't appear to be in any distress. Looking at her, I cursed my overactive imagination, thinking I could have been sitting in front of the fire by now if only I had left well enough alone. Hopefully, it would be only a matter of a quick pull and I'd be on my way again. I felt happier as I placed my gloved hand into the swollen vagina.

In a job as unpredictable as large-animal veterinary, it's normally a lovely feeling when your gut instincts prove to be right, but this time, I would have been delighted to be wrong. With a sense of dread, I felt the tense bands of tissue sweeping off in a tight circle. I could just fit my fingers in through the narrow opening, to feel two enormous cloven hooves. As I prodded at the sensitive tissue between the feet, I felt the indignant twitch of the calf who was probably wondering what was going on.

'Well, you were right to be worried, Gerry. I'm afraid she has a twisted uterus.'

'What the hell is that?' he enquired, looking puzzled. 'I've come across a few things in my time but I've never come across one of those!'

'Well, count yourself lucky. It normally happens with a big calf like this one and, for whatever reason, the whole womb twists over on itself, leaving only a very narrow opening, so the calf can't get out.'

'Sounds like a hopeless case then. Is she a lost cause?'

'Hopefully not. But there's no denying it's a messy job. What we'll have to try and do is get her down on the ground and roll her over – hopefully then the uterus will twist back into place. If that doesn't work, then we'll have to do a caesarean. But that's not an easy job either with a cow like this. Either way we're going to need a bit of muscle power, though. Any neighbours we could root out?'

'We can do better than that for you. John and Robert, my two sons, are up in the house. I'll give them a shout.'

I couldn't dispel the feeling of dread as I made my way back to the jeep to get my sedative and the ropes that I'd need to cast the cow. I had by now learnt the hard way that performing a procedure was never as straightforward as it sounded.

I was somewhat relieved to see Gerry coming back from the house flanked by his two strapping sons. They definitely looked like they might come in handy.

'What do you want us to do?' asked Robert, who wouldn't have looked out of place in the front row of a scrum.

'If you could just grab hold of her, please, while I give her a sedative shot, that would be great.'

I drew up a small dose, just enough to take the edge off her. She didn't stand a chance as Robert towered over her, enormous arms encircling her head while he held her by the nose. I quickly tied two ropes around her body, thanking God that I had managed to make it to that practical in college. At least I could start the job looking like I knew what I was doing.

'This looks a bit like a cowboy and Indian film,' said John, the younger son, as the cow stood snorting in disgust to find herself unable to move against the ropes. With Robert holding her head and Gerry, John and myself pulling steadily on the rope from behind, the cow slowly sank to the ground with surprisingly little resistance. So far so good.

'This is where the fun starts!' I said to the three men, explaining how they would have to roll the cow over from one side to the other as I lay on the ground, with my hand against the uterus inside the cow. If the situation hadn't been quite so desperate, I would have been amused by my compromising position as I lay, face down in the muddy straw, hanging out of a cow's rear end with three enormous men cheering me on encouragingly.

As soon as I had myself in position, I called out, 'Right, now, flip her over!', wondering how many times I would have to repeat the scenario before admitting defeat and scrubbing up for a caesarean.

With an enormous lurch, I felt the cow heaving over, unable to resist the brute force. I pushed against the dead weight of the uterus and just as the cow flipped over, I felt an unmistakable squelch as the uterus slipped away from my hands and a gush of fluid poured out from the vagina. I took a few deep breaths, allowing the numbness in my arms to recover and then gingerly had a feel.

I couldn't believe it – everything felt perfect.

The two feet were now in place in the vagina, followed by a large head. Although it was a big calf, the cow was broad and roomy, and I was confident that I would get him out easily enough with a bit of help and patience.

'What's the story, will we try again?' asked John, starting to warm to the job.

'Oh no, not at all. Everything's fine now. That did the trick,' I replied airily, hoping they wouldn't be able to hear my heart which was still thumping in disbelief.

'God, that's great. I thought it would have been a bigger job than that,' replied Gerry. 'You must have done a right few of them before.'

'Well, you know, some of them are easier than others, Gerry,' I replied non-committally.

Before long, the calf's forelegs and head were visible and the tiny nose twitched with impatience after his long wait.

'He's alive and all!' shouted Gerry, delighted with the outcome.

Soon the huge bull calf had been delivered and lay shivering at his mother's nose, none the worse for wear. The cow seemed a little surprised by his arrival and sniffed him warily as though wondering where the little creature had come from. I held my breath and then relaxed as she began to lick him with increasing vigour. As Robert went up to help rub him down, she shook her head angrily at him and I knew that all would be well.

'You'll have to come in for a cup of tea after all that,' said Gerry, clearly delighted with the result.

I happily agreed. By the time I had washed my instruments and peeled off the mucky overalls, a fine spread was laid out on the kitchen table. The successful outcome of such a potentially daunting job was enough to put me in a good mood which was only enhanced as my plate was piled high with an assortment of home-made breads and cheese followed by hot apple tart and freshly whipped cream. It took a few mugs of hot tea to wash it all down. As I sat chatting with the family, I realised this was the part that made it all worthwhile. The hospitality shown to me by many farmers was just second to none. There couldn't be many professions where such appreciation was shown for a job well done.

CHAPTER TWENTY-ONE

DOCTORS AND VETS

One of my sisters studied medicine at UCD, and was already a surgical intern when I started at veterinary college. By the time I qualified, she had risen to the rank of specialist registrar in orthopaedic surgery. We got on very well and often spent an evening in the pub comparing case notes. In some ways, the similarities between our chosen professions were remarkable; in others they couldn't have been further apart.

'So, what did you do when you realised that the horse had a twisted gut?' she would ask, taking a swig of her black rum and Coke.

'Sure, I had to shoot him,' I replied dolefully. 'The owner had no money and, even if he had, I don't think the horse would have survived the journey to the referral hospital.'

Often, I would be in the middle of telling her some tale when I would notice her incredulous face as she pictured me doing the best I could in some arduous circumstances.

She made gallant attempts to hide her shocked reactions to some of my more vivid descriptions of the various emergency situations I had encountered.

'Why couldn't you have referred the bullock to one of the hospitals,' she would ask, 'instead of just slashing him open in the field in the middle of the night without any help?'

'But they'd never pay for that! Sure, he was worth very little by then,' I would answer lamely. Luckily, the expression 'economically viable' doesn't register in the world of human medicine.

Such scenarios became more complicated where pets were involved. Ongoing advances in veterinary medicine meant that new treatment options were constantly becoming available, especially in the case of 'companion animals'. More and more, we found that our clients were becoming familiar with new procedures from sources such as the internet and popular veterinary programmes on television. However, these programmes often failed to mention the price of such a level of care, which in many cases would be beyond the budget of the average pet-owner. When owners couldn't afford the expensive procedures which we were increasingly able to offer, it was left to the practitioner to carry out what could only be described as a 'salvage procedure'.

'You don't mean to say you amputated his leg when he only had a fractured talus with a dislocated hock?' my sister would ask in amazement (after my brief sketch of the anatomy of the joint on a beer mat).

She particularly found it hard to believe that straight out

of college you were expected to be able to do more or less any job on hand without any backup. 'So you just washed your hands and started cutting the cow open, despite the fact you'd *never* done a caesarean before?!'

I think she was slightly jealous, if truth be told. After one year out of college, I had probably got more 'hands-on experience' in surgery than she had gained in her years of intensive training. Of course, I wouldn't like to start comparing success rates or mortality rates and I'm glad I never had to operate on a human. The trial-and-error principle isn't always very satisfactory when it comes to surgery.

It took my sister a while to stop asking questions like: 'Why didn't you send him for a brain scan?' or 'Why didn't you put him in the intensive care unit instead of leaving him lying in a kennel?'

One night, having described to her how frustrated I was by my lack of equipment, I opened the back of my jeep to show her my array of drugs and instruments.

'This is my hospital,' I said. 'This is all I have.'

I was glad she didn't notice the humane-killer lying in its pouch under the car seat.

Often *I* envied *her* her job as she would describe a night in the trauma unit: 'Well, we weren't sure how severe the damage was, so I sent him off for an MRI scan. When that came back, we decided to operate, so I rang the consultant and then the anaesthetists came in to get him ready. When the consultant and I had finished on his orthopaedic injuries, we called in the plastics team and went off for coffee. We spoke to the relations after. They were so grateful to us.'

I would nod knowingly, mentally converting the scenario into the veterinary equivalent: 'Well, I wasn't sure how severe the damage was so I just hoped for the best and gave him a shot of steroids. The owner said the last bill he'd got from us was a bloody joke – imagine charging fifty euro to calve a cow at night! – and he bloody well wasn't going to pay this time. I decided I'd have to operate on the bullock but I'd never done it before so I rang my boss to ask him if he could give me a hand and he told me to get stuffed, he was in the pub. So I just got on with it as best I could, knowing the farmer had no intention of paying the bill anyway. When I finally left the yard at half-past one in the morning, having spent another hour stitching up the animal's wounds after I'd finished treating the other injuries, the farmer told me all bloody vets were a waste of time anyway and he didn't know why he'd bothered to call me out in the first place.'

But despite all that, I wouldn't have swapped jobs with her for all the money in the world. At the end of the day, as a vet I was dealing with animals and the worst that could happen would be a very upset owner or a court summons with the Veterinary Defence Society to defend me.

At times, my sister would describe cases where she and the medical team would be dealing with young men left paralysed for life after a motorbike injury, or a young mother or child dying on the surgical table. Matters of life and death took on a whole other dimension in her job.

It is amazing the number of people who have said to me that a vet must be better than any doctor because we study so many species of animal and have to do everything – no referring of patients off to the specialists. In ways, they are right, but they forget one simple point. Although we do indeed study many different species of animal, we don't study the human one.

Even so, it was not uncommon for me to arrive out on a call to a yard and be asked: 'Oh, while you're here you couldn't ever check my wife's leg? She went down to the doctor yesterday but those people know nothing. She'd be much happier if you had a look at it.' I would politely decline, explaining that our veterinary insurance didn't extend to carrying out nixers on humans.

Despite the differences between our professions, my sister and I would often find it useful to check things with each other. Once she rang me from casualty wondering what sort of antibiotic would be suitable for a farmer who had stabbed himself with a silage fork. The correct one was totally different to what the consultant had prescribed – in his blissful urban ignorance he didn't know that silage was acidic. On another occasion, she rang about a child who had been bitten by a sheep and now had an unusual-looking growth on her finger. I was immediately able to diagnose orf – a common viral infection in sheep that is contagious to humans.

Once I rang her during one of our regular 'salvage' jobs to see what sort of pins and screws would be best to repair a shattered femur in a collie. Having got the necessary dimensions, I went off to Woodies to find a cheaper equivalent!

Sometimes, having access to the type of equipment used in human medicine would be a huge boon for vets.

One night, my sister explained to me about the saws they used to remove plaster casts in children. The saw was like an ordinary saw but had the distinguishing feature of being sensitive to human tissue so the blade wouldn't cut through flesh. This could be a great advancement in our attempts at cast removal, I thought, which were generally slow and painstaking as we took great care not to cut into the delicate tissues of the animal's leg. The job was so tedious that it often influenced how much casting material you would put on in the first place. Unless you knew that someone else was going to take it off, you held back on putting on too much.

'No, believe me,' I once explained to a farmer, whose bull calf needed an extra-large quantity. 'The cast must come off on Wednesday the twelfth – not a day sooner or later.' I knew that I was going to a conference in Dublin that day and so one of the others would have to carry out the tiresome procedure!

When I heard about my sister's saw, I put in an order for one from her immediately. Luckily, there was a delay in getting it. She rang me from work one evening to tell me about a very small and frightened child who came in to have her cast removed from her arm. Every time the doctor turned the saw on, she shrieked and yelled and refused to let him near her. She clutched her Winnie the Pooh teddy bear and buried her head in her mother's arms.

Eventually the doctor got frustrated, not wanting to have to put her through an anaesthetic for such a simple procedure. He fancied himself as being good with children and eventually managed to persuade her to hand over Winnie the Pooh to demonstrate that it didn't hurt. As he ran the saw up and down the teddy bear's arm, all was going well and the little girl was nearly ready to follow her brave bear's example. Then one of the threads in the teddy's arm caught in the saw and Winnie the Pooh was promptly shredded into dozens of tiny pieces, sending puffs of saw-dust and red clothing in all directions. I never heard if they managed to get the plaster off the child but I decided that I would probably be safer not to experiment with the wonder saw because of the similarities of texture between many of our patients and that of Winnie the Pooh!

When I qualified as a veterinary surgeon my sister gave me a present of a hardback book, grandly titled *An Atlas of Veterinary Surgery*. Inside she inscribed it with words that just about summed up the differences in our jobs: '*Best wishes in your future career!! Hope this is occasionally useful as an alternative to a bullet in the head.*'

CHAPTER TWENTY-TWO

MENFOLK

E ven though I had qualified as a veterinary surgeon just before the onset of the twenty-first century, life as a mixed-animal vet was still, to a large extent, dominated by men. This state of affairs didn't particularly worry me. Like anything, it had its advantages and disadvantages, and you just had to make the most of it. It often amused me when farmers insisted on catching or holding an animal for me. I think they expected less of the 'more delicate sex' and, to be perfectly honest, it suited me just fine – I didn't feel the need to prove to myself or to anyone else that I was better than any man. If it meant I had less work to do, I wasn't going to object!

During my student years, I had become accustomed to farmers bringing out a basin of hot water, an unopened bar of soap and a crisp, clean towel for my benefit while the male vet was expected to hose down under a cold tap. I felt I could put up with such discrimination.

I don't know whether it was because I was a female, or

because of some half-starved look I had about me, but I rarely left any place without being offered vast quantities of refreshments, which I availed of on a regular basis.

Of course, being female didn't always work to my advantage; some farmers seemed to have a particular problem with the whole concept of a female vet. Even in cases where everything worked out beautifully, and I regularly saved their animals from the jaws of death, they failed to be impressed. Needless to say, if anything ever went wrong, I was the biggest waste of space ever created. But I became a thick-skinned waste of space.

One of the most notorious offenders in this regard was a farmer by the name of Wayne McLoughlin. What made him worse was the fact that he was not only young, but also well-educated. I could forgive the ageing bachelors, who had farmed for generations while the nearest their womenfolk got to the farm was feeding the calves or the hens. Equally, I could forgive the younger hill farmers who had barely completed any formal education and lived in the few remaining remote pockets where even women going into pubs was still frowned upon. But Wayne had no such excuse. He was in his early thirties and had been reared on a progressive dairy farm. After school, he had gone to UCD and completed a degree in agricultural science. I don't know how he had got on with his female colleagues but obviously they had left no favourable impression on him – certainly not in an academic sense anyway.

The first time I met him, I observed a tall, powerfully built man striding across the yard with a welcoming smile.

He was obviously admiring the jeep. As I opened the door and stepped out, the smile dropped from his face.

'Oh for God's sake, not another bloody female vet!'

'I don't believe it,' I retorted cheerfully, 'not another male farmer!' My sarcasm was lost on him, however.

'This is a good pedigree cow of mine. She needs a caesarean and I don't want her messed around.'

I'm always ready to admit that a lot of farmers have more experience than I do, but it really annoys me when I'm told what to do. Caesarean sections in cows are something that are demanded on a regular basis when somebody panics. I've often noticed that the most educated farmers are the most inclined to do this. But it's not an operation to be undertaken lightly. Of course there are occasions where there is no alternative but, in many cases, with a little bit of patience in giving a young heifer a chance to get on with the job, or with a bit of careful manipulation, it can be avoided.

I've always noticed that the farmers who are the most vocal in demanding a caesarean are the ones most likely to complain when the job is done and the panic over. 'Not much of a calf, is he? A bit of a pull would have done that lad and saved us a big bill.'

After one particularly bad call – partly my fault, but also strongly influenced by an irate farmer – I decided to rely on my own judgement in future. That way, if things went wrong, I only had myself to blame.

* * *

On this particular day Wayne snorted irately as I pulled on a pair of rectaling gloves and applied a liberal quantity of lubricating gel.

'I'm telling you, she's for a caesarean,' he stated. 'She hasn't made any progress for the last hour and I've had a feel inside her.'

'Well, if you wouldn't mind, I'd like to have a feel for myself.'

I thrust my hand deep into the heifer's vagina, ignoring the impatient sighs and the eyes rolled up to heaven behind me. Although she had the narrow hip conformation of a typical Friesian heifer, she was relatively roomy in relation to the size of the calf. I was fairly confident that I could calve her without too much of a pull.

'I think we'll get it out with the jack,' I informed the disbelieving Wayne. 'There's no point in putting a good heifer through a section unnecessarily.'

'This is bloody ridiculous. I'm telling you, you'll damage her with the jack. Are you trying to tell me I don't know my own bloody job?'

'No. In fact, *you're* trying to tell me I don't know *mine*,' I replied calmly. 'I'm not sectioning this heifer.'

'This is unbelievable. Well, on your head be it. Your boss will be hearing about this when it goes wrong.'

'I'm sure,' I muttered to myself as I took the calving ropes out of their container.

The job took just fifteen minutes, most of which time was spent in relaxing the heifer and allowing her own contractions to deliver the calf with a little bit of help from the jack. The bull calf shook his head in surprise at his undignified entry into a strange new world. I was delighted as the heifer began to sniff at the ungainly little creature with a look of bewilderment. She was none the worse for wear.

'You were bloody lucky this time,' was the only comment from Wayne.

During all future calls I did at McLoughlin's, nothing ever went wrong. It was one of those rare yards where, no matter what I did, it seemed to work. Yet Wayne always insisted on berating my best efforts and I continually had to put up with his 'bloody female vet!' comments.

I usually tried to avoid the yard, but one morning I scanned down the list of jobs in the office and saw a call to W. McLoughlin, Ashford, to castrate a young bull. Arthur had scribbled his name beside it, indicating that he would do it. When he came in, I turned to him.

'Listen, I see you have your name down for McLoughlin's, but I'll be out that way testing just beforehand so I might as well do it to save you the drive.'

'If you would, that'd be great. I've those two horses to vet out in McDonald's and a mare to scan on the way back. It would really take the pressure off me. I just didn't want to put you down for it because I know he isn't exactly your favourite client.'

'Ah, just think how much it will make me appreciate all the others then,' I replied grimly.

* * *

'I thought Arthur was coming out.'

I hadn't expected any niceties from Wayne. None of the usual casual chat about the weather or the rate of the grass growth. 'No, he was too busy. You'll have to do with me instead, but don't worry, it's a simple little job. Two quick snips and it's all over. I'm sure even a female vet can manage that.'

'Well, this bull is going for sale in three weeks so I don't want him going back on me. Have you ever done one of these before?'

'Oh believe me, I've done plenty – many more than you could ever imagine!'

He glared at me. A sense of humour was not one of his strong points.

In fairness, in terms of equipment, Wayne was always well set up and I was glad to notice the strong crush containing my patient. The bull didn't look like the type you would mess around with. I fervently hoped that he wouldn't guess my intentions.

He glared malevolently at me with an expression he might have borrowed from his owner, as I sedated him. While I waited for the sedation to take effect, I carefully scrubbed and disinfected the surgical site. Having injected him with antibiotics and anti-tetanus, I then drew up a measure of local anaesthetic to inject into both testicles.

'Now, get a good hold of the tail, please. This might sting a bit.' I enjoyed watching Wayne wincing as the bull snorted in reaction to my administrations.

Normally the time spent waiting for the anaesthetic to work is passed in idle chat with the farmers – not so with

Wayne, but I wasn't going to let him away with it this time. I'd had enough of his sullen silences.

'Isn't this a really beautiful piece of craftsmanship?' I began as I unwrapped the emasculators which we used to crush the vessel supplying the testicles. 'Look at the way all five jaws lock so perfectly into each other. There's no way any self-respecting testicle could overcome that.'

Wayne shifted uncomfortably from one foot to another. Like many supposedly tough farmers, he took pride in his total lack of squeamishness, but a threat to one's manhood was a different matter, especially from a no-hoper female.

'You know, it's one of the most expensive instruments we have,' I continued conversationally, 'but it's worth every penny. It does such an efficient job. I always feel it's a job well done.'

'Do you think you could just get on with it? I haven't all day to waste.' I noticed his tone had lost some of its usual arrogance despite his gruff words.

'Oh, absolutely, if you'd prefer. It's just that normally, I like to give plenty of time for the anaesthetic to work. It must be so horrifically painful. But no, you're right. We don't want to stand around all day. I'm sure he'll get over it.'

I noticed Wayne's firm hold on the tail weaken slightly as I slashed a long incision deep into each testicle. I'm not really cruel by nature and honestly, the bull didn't feel a thing as I had, in fact, given ample time for the local anaesthetic to take effect. The testicles dropped neatly out of their containing sack, suspended by the thick vasculature of a mature bull. Wayne was beginning to look a bit ashen-faced by this stage in the proceedings.

'You wouldn't be embarrassed to own those!' I said cheerfully, but got no reply.

'Now for the fun part,' I said viciously. I opened wide the jaws of the gleaming emasculators and placed them carefully around the vast blood-supply. With great enthusiasm, I closed the enormous jaws and enjoyed the loud crunch, followed by a gentle thud as the offending article dropped harmlessly to the ground, having been severed by the final blade.

I opened my mouth to give further encouragement to my assistant only to be interrupted by a much louder thump. I turned and saw that Wayne had slumped gracelessly to the ground. For a second, I considered propping him up in the recovery position but on reflection decided that I really couldn't be bothered. I felt slightly disappointed that the show was now over.

I tied the bull's tail up to the side bar of the crush, rescrubbed and continued with the job without my audience. By the time I had finished, Wayne had come round and managed to scramble to his feet. He made a few attempts to bend over, as though searching for whatever he was pretending he had dropped on the ground, but he knew I wasn't convinced. He returned my sympathetic smile with a menacing scowl that somehow didn't carry the same impact as usual, given how pale he now looked. He didn't open his mouth again, and I left the yard grinning happily, satisfied with another job well done.

CHAPTER TWENTY-THREE

AN UNUSUAL CASE

A nd then there were the glorious days; the days that you replayed over and over again in your mind to convince yourself that, one day, you just might become a worthy member of the veterinary profession, after all. The fact that the success was due to a combination of good fortune and being in the right place at the right time, became totally irrelevant.

It didn't seem like it was shaping up to be one of those days when I stepped out of the shower that morning to find eleven missed calls on the phone. I pulled a towel around me before listening to a garbled message about a bleeding horse, collapsed in a stable. As is often the case in an emergency, the owner of the voice had neglected to leave me such vaguely useful information as his name or telephone number. I was briefly grateful to Eircom as I hit the last-caller button. The phone was answered on the first ring.

'He's down in the box and there's blood everywhere and he's in an awful bad way. How soon can you get here?'

I patiently extracted the relevant information as I wondered if I had by any chance missed the opening part of the conversation.

I felt out of breath myself by the time I hung up but I still wasn't terribly concerned. A bleeding horse invariably looks worse than it really is to an owner and I felt confident enough about having to deal with a simple stitch-up job. I mentally prepared myself for the soothing talk with the client, the carefully administered sedative to the trembling horse, the thorough flushing of the injury, and I was almost congratulating myself on the neat row of sutures by the time I pulled into the yard. Stepping out of the jeep, I pulled on a warm jacket as, seemingly overnight, summer had given way to autumn and the ground was covered in a crisp frost.

Owen O'Malley was a hefty man and he looked all of his eighteen stone as he puffed down from the stables to meet me.

'I thought you'd got lost,' he said. 'Archie is out of a Clover Hill mare. He won the heavy hunter class in the RDS this year and I've a good buyer waiting for him as soon as he passes the vet. No chance of that now – even if you can save him,' he added ominously.

I tried not to look smug as I followed him up the uneven ground to the row of immaculate loose-boxes, anticipating how good I was going to look when Archie was sound and ready for sale in a week's time. But my confidence quickly evaporated as the narrow ray of light that illuminated the dark box revealed a handsome hunter lying pathetically on the fresh bed of straw. Before I could stop him, Owen went in and grabbed hold of the head-collar.

'Get up, Archie. Come on, get up,' he implored the horse, pulling until the horse's head and neck were up off the ground. As soon as he let the head-collar go, Archie slumped lifelessly back on to the straw.

An ice-cold shudder shot up my spine as I realised this was no ordinary cut horse. Without realising that I was holding my breath, I followed the fresh blood on the straw to the site of the wound and then stopped, perplexed. A ragged gash was visible, just above the fetlock, under a mass of blood-stained hair, but things just didn't add up. The cut, while significant in its own way, could not possibly account for the animal's collapsed state. For once, my old college lecturer's much repeated addendum of 'common things are common' just didn't ring true.

As is usual when I have absolutely no idea what to say, I busied myself with a careful examination of the heart and lungs to give me some time to think.

'He must have bled all night,' said Owen, interrupting my frenzied thought. 'I found him up the top field and he was so weak that I only just about managed to get him down to the box before he collapsed on me. There can't be any blood left in him, at all.'

'That's where you're wrong, Owen,' I replied, feeling as though my voice was coming from a long distance away. 'It's not a bad cut at all and that amount of blood loss shouldn't worry a cat never mind a great big animal like him. And look at this!' I exclaimed, as I pulled up Archie's top lip to reveal a congested, mucky-looking mucous membrane. 'There's more going on here than just a simple cut, Owen. I just don't know what to make of him. I really don't know.'

'Do you think you can stitch him then?' he replied, completely missing the point. I carefully auscultated the abdomen, listening expectantly for the intermittent grumbling and trickling that would assure me all was well. I tapped carefully on the head of the stethoscope, thinking it wasn't working right, as all I could hear was the dull, sluggish leaking of an unenthusiastic gut. Not your usual colic, I thought to myself, but a sure sign that something was amiss. I leaned up against the wall of the stable, with my hands to my head, wondering what on earth was going on, and stared blankly at the limp animal. His shallow, measured breathing was definitely not that of the typical colicky horse, which would be writhing and thrashing in pain.

I stood there for God knows how long, gazing cluelessly into the horse's glazed eye. As I watched, he carelessly stretched his neck and pulled out a wisp of hay from the pile that lay in the corner of the box. The silence was broken only by his methodical chomping. I was puzzled. How could an animal, so obviously ill, be interested in food? And that was when it started to come to me, like a light beginning to dawn on a far horizon. Somewhere in the recesses of my brain I recalled a similar situation – a lifeless horse but with the same wistful chewing of hay. And looking back to my patient, I could see there were other similarities. Archie was not in any pain. In fact, if I were to hazard a guess, I would go so far as to say he was quite relaxed. In fact, even a bit mellow. I stared at the vacant expression on the horse, noted again his regular, shallow breathing and looked back at the mucky colour of his membranes, and then in one fantastic instant, it all made sense.

'Owen,' I said, 'the field you took him out of. Were there any wild mushrooms in it?'

Many years previously, while 'seeing practice', the vet I had been accompanying had come across a case on a frosty October morning where two horses were found stretched out in a field, unable to rise and obviously dying, but with no obvious cause. Although, at the time, I had no idea quite what was going on, I vividly remembered the day spent in vain, sending off samples for analysis and treating the horses symptomatically until the next morning when they both gave up the battle and died. As far as I knew, the real cause of death was never confirmed by any laboratory but a similar spate of cases had occurred within the same week, and all within a clearly defined area. The only logical explanation was that, following specific seasonal conditions, a certain type of mushroom had grown and, after the short spell of frost which always preceded these cases, the mushroom in question became palatable to horses. This then gave rise to multiple cases, over a couple of days, of what was assumed to be mushroom poisoning. All through my college years I tried to find out more about this condition, but not once did I come across a single reference to it. Now, here I was, working in the same area where those cases had occurred and I was fully convinced that what I was dealing with was indeed a case of mushroom poisoning.

Despite my enthusiasm at having stumbled across such

an obscure case, Owen remained sceptical as I gave him a garbled explanation of my diagnosis.

'And are you sure it's not all the blood he lost from the cut that has him so weak in himself?' he asked dubiously.

'Absolutely sure!' I replied. 'I know it sounds crazy, but even though it's years since I saw it, the look in his eyes is so characteristic that I'm sure this is what we're dealing with. The cut is incidental. He probably did it staggering around the field.'

My heart missed a beat as Owen, sounding a lot happier than he had up to now, asked the next question.

'Well, now that we know what we're dealing with, how do we cure him?'

'I'm afraid it's not that simple at all,' I replied slowly. 'In the cases I heard about – eight in all – most of them died and, of the ones that recovered, one had to be put down a year later because of chronic kidney failure. There is no antidote and, even with intensive treatment, these cases seem to be fairly hopeless. I'm sorry, Owen, but it's not looking good for him.' I watched in silence as he tried to take in what I was saying.

I tried desperately to come up with a solution. 'I'll tell you what, if we get him into a box, I can refer him to one of the equine hospitals as he's such a valuable horse, and see what they can do,' I began, rapidly warming to the idea of washing my hands of a case that I knew was out of my league. However, that idea didn't last long as I rang one after another of the top hospitals who all suggested euthanasia, although some were slightly sceptical about my diagnosis.

'And have you treated horses at all yourself before, or is it just the small animals you're used to?' asked one of the specialists to whom I spoke.

I didn't bother to reply.

'Is there really nothing to be done?' asked Owen as I relayed the messages back to him.

I stood looking at the powerful hunter, lying prostrate in the box, gazing stupidly into space and I, no more than Owen, could not stomach the idea of putting an end to him without a fight.

'Well,' I began hesitantly, 'I don't like to throw good money after bad, but if you really want, we can try to keep him going and see if he can clear the poison.' My voice trailed off, knowing that what I was suggesting was ludicrous, but Owen instantly jumped at the idea.

'That's what I was hoping you would say. I don't like pushing you into it but, to be honest, I'd rather you treat him than any of those hospitals. I reckon if you're good enough to know what's wrong with Archie, you're good enough to save him.'

Instantly, I regretted my suggestion, but once Owen had got the idea into his head, there was no going back and, before I knew it, I was down on my knees infusing litre after litre of saline into the horse's vein, hoping to dilute and flush out the toxin. Desperately, I sorted through the cases of drugs in my jeep, hoping to be inspired as to what to give the horse. I added a diuretic into the saline drip and then I injected him with some supplements that at least could do no harm.

The day passed in a blur as I revisited the patient hourly

to adjust his fluids and check on his condition. He seemed to be totally oblivious to my presence but continued to chew dreamily on the sweet meadow hay without even lifting his head. Shortly after midday, a stream of red-tinted urine flowed from him as I sat by, helplessly wondering how an innocuous-looking mushroom could do such horrendous damage to six hundred kilos of well-made horse. To pass the time, I stitched and bandaged the cut that had caused Owen so much initial concern. At each visit, I reminded him of the hopelessness of the case but, each time I returned, a quick glance at his face assured me that we hadn't lost yet.

The day ran into night and I carried on with no apparent change in Archie's condition. Then, just as I was beginning to give up and when even Owen's enthusiasm seemed to be waning, a miracle happened. Having gone into the house for a quick cup of tea and a sandwich, we returned to the box, and then I was sure that the condition was contagious and that I myself was hallucinating – because there before me stood Archie, staggering slightly, head drooped and totally oblivious to the twenty-four-hour emergency that he had caused.

It was late when I got home and Donal had already gone to bed. He must have thought he was dreaming as I filled him in on all the details, oblivious to the fact that he had been sleeping peacefully until my arrival.

I called into the yard early the next morning and, apart from the bandage on his left fore, Archie looked almost normal. The weeks and the months passed and still I waited for the inevitable kidney failure, but repeated blood tests showed perfectly healthy kidney and liver functions.

I can't quite explain why or how he recovered and, to be honest, I can take absolutely no credit for it because the treatment I used was purely an imitation of what I had seen done before when all the horses died. I've given up trying to explain to Owen that the only reason Archie lived is either that he ate so little of the mushroom that it wasn't enough to kill him, or that it was a slightly different type of mushroom from the one that had killed the other horses. I am, however, sure of my diagnosis because I heard that another case occurred, not five miles away, that same weekend.

I've seen Archie, or 'Archibald's Pride' as he's better known in showing circles, competing at shows a few times since and, although I know the credit is totally misplaced, I can't help grinning to myself when I see Owen propping up the bar, relaying the usual story.

'And all the others died!' he exclaims, taking another swig of his pint before the enraptured audience. 'And every equine hospital said to put Archie down, but no, my vet knew better than the rest of them!'

CHAPTER TWENTY-FOUR

THE MATCHMAKER

It had been a long day but for once I didn't mind having to do an extra call on the way home. The Roches lived high up in the Wicklow mountains, near Glendalough. I had purposely left their call until now, so that when finished, instead of heading back down the mountain, I could continue my journey out over the Sally Gap towards home. At this time of year I might even catch a glimpse of the deer that came down from the high mountains, or hear the high-pitched, lonely whistle of a rutting stag.

The Roches were of a dying breed. Mrs Roche, now becoming increasingly blind, had married into the rough twenty-acre holding high up on the side of the Wicklow mountains. How she and her husband had managed to eke out a living from the rocky landscape, not only for themselves but also for their five sons, was beyond comprehension. Sitting in the crowded kitchen, drinking a cup of hot tea with them, you could get no sense of the hardship and sacrifices they must have undergone in their lifetime. In one way, it was a good thing that changing agricultural practices had eliminated a lot of the toil and slog of farming, but sad too to think that intensification had also wiped out an entire generation of these small hill farmers.

As I pulled into the driveway, I gazed lazily out the window at the mountain ewes grazing at ease alongside an assortment of crossbred Hereford cattle. Amongst them lumbered the old Saddleback sow. She earned her keep by using up the household waste and producing litters of shiny-coated black-and-white bonhams on a regular basis.

The sons, now well into middle age, had maintained the farm to keep their parents happy. Although in their eighties, both Mr and Mrs Roche had retained a strong interest in everything that went on in the farm and arguments broke out on a regular basis between father and sons about the ongoing management, giving rise to situations where I ended up acting as reluctant mediator. Of the two sons who still lived at home, one worked as a building contractor while the other worked late shifts in one of the large drug companies that employed most of the farmers' sons in the area. There was no way that their meagre collection of animals could ever support such a large family.

The first time I went up to them was in mid-February and heavy sleet accompanied my arrival. I was greeted by Mrs Roche who seemed to be permanently in the doorway, as though waiting. When I had introduced myself as the new assistant, she quickly ushered me into the cosy kitchen and pushed a mug of steaming tea into my hands.

'Let the men carry on with the work out there,' she began. 'That rough yard is no place for a lady such as yourself on a day like this.'

'Thanks very much, Mrs Roche, but I'd better go out and get on with the job as soon as I've had the tea. I've a good few places to get to yet.'

'You'll do no such thing! Sure, won't Fergus call in for you when he's ready to go.'

Yet again, I had to explain that, unbelievable and all as it apparently was, I genuinely was the vet.

'Fergus left the practice after Christmas, Mrs Roche. He and his wife have moved to Kildare. I'm Seamus's new assistant.'

The look of confusion on her face had nothing to do with her partial blindness, and she spent the next twenty minutes trying to convince me that I had made a drastic mistake.

'You see, the boys have a bit of a rough job to do. Not a job a lady such as yourself could carry out.'

The call was to 'squeeze' or bloodlessly emasculate six bulls.

'Don't worry, Mrs Roche, I've done it many times before. It's not such a hard job.' As the minutes ticked away on the wooden clock perched on the shelf above the old range, I was beginning to get restless. Just then, Joe and Tony arrived in from the yard. They had heard the jeep pulling up and were wondering what the delay was. They both nodded respectfully at me as Joe declared, 'We're ready to start if Fergus is around.' The explanations began all over again.

Joe was beginning to wonder if maybe the weather was turning a bit rough and, anyway, he didn't think the bulls were really quite strong enough yet – sure, maybe he'd let them go another week or two. I decided enough was enough. Without another word, I made my way out the door and over to the crush, brandishing my gleaming burdizzo.

'Now, if you could just get a good hold of the tail, please, we'll be finished in no time,' I instructed as authoritively as I could. Both sons shook their heads doubtfully but did as instructed. A few indignant bawls later and it was all over.

Over the few months that followed, I always seemed to be the one on duty when the Roches required attention. Gradually, they got used to the novel idea. While in the yard, I was usually accompanied by either Tony or Joe, as old Mr Roche was becoming increasingly arthritic and the bitter winter winds that swept around the hillside farm set him off into spasms of coughing whenever he did venture outside. After the sons' initial embarrassment turned into gentle, good-humoured slagging, I began to enjoy the visits. I knew I had finally been accepted when Joe confided in me one day: 'D'you know, Gillian, the animals always seem to get better when you treat them!' I tried not to take offence at his surprise.

Mrs Roche insisted on thinking of me as a lady, despite occasionally witnessing situations where my behaviour hardly qualified as decorous. I was quite sure, too, that her sharp hearing had picked up some of my less than ladylike reactions to the antics of their unruly animals.

I was becoming accustomed to the hospitality of the country folk in the area, but it took me a while to figure out why the kindly mother was so attentive to my every need. A simple job could take over an hour as there was no way that it would ever be carried out without first sitting down to the copious dinner that had always been freshly cooked for my arrival. Equally, having finished whatever routine little task I had been called upon to perform, I would be escorted, despite my protestations, back into the kitchen to top up with a few mugs of hot tea and assorted platefuls of home-made biscuits. On staggering, bloated, back to the jeep, I would usually find Slug zealously guarding half a dozen eggs or a freshly baked tea brack.

One day, Mrs Roche casually mentioned that one of her neighbour's sons had got married the previous week. 'There's no greater comfort to any mother than to see her sons well married,' she stated.

It was then that it finally struck me: Mrs Roche was a woman with a mission.

The sons, obviously used to their mother's methods, enjoyed encouraging her in her wild illusions and, from that day on, I couldn't arrive into the kitchen without Joe or Tony casually dropping some ingenious comment like, 'So, I heard you won the scone-making competition in the village festival last week, Gillian,' or 'How do you possibly find the time to run that local youth club as well as knitting for the Bosnian appeal?'

Mrs Roche positively glowed with the growing conviction that a match had been made in heaven.

My best attempts to put the record straight by casually

alluding to my husband were to no avail as they were always greeted by the sons with guffaws of laughter. 'Would you listen to her – pretending to be married! Sure, she's only making that up in case some auld farmer might get fancy notions about himself!' The winks and nudges went unnoticed by Mrs Roche with her failing sight.

When Donal and I happened to meet up with Joe and Tony and one of the other brothers, Michael, one night, I thought that things might improve. I introduced them to Donal amidst much merriment and good-natured slagging on both sides.

'Well, sure, if you have a bit of land, lads, I'm sure we could come up with some sort of a deal,' joked Donal, who was in on the story.

* * *

I was rudely awoken by Slug from my daydream as I sat looking at the Roche farmyard. She had suddenly been roused out of her cosy slumber by the indignant squeals of the latest litter of bonhams running around the yard. The noise had interrupted her dreams, in which, no doubt, she had been enjoying a hot-blooded chase. She hit the windscreen with a flurry of throaty barks.

I laughingly shouted at her: 'Sit down and behave yourself! It's not your dinner.' Old habits die hard but she nonetheless reluctantly returned to her seat, aggrieved by my unsporting nature.

Tony appeared around the corner, having heard the racket and knowing exactly who had caused it. I cringed with embarrassment thinking of the time some months before when I had been busy scanning a mare in the yard. The noisy quacks of the yard ducks had failed to alert anyone's attention. It wasn't until Slug came around the corner proudly dragging the limp body of the biggest drake that I realised she had jumped out the car window.

'She's at it again! Would you ever go and feed that dog!' called Tony as I got out of the car. 'You'd better go in to Mother. She has your dinner ready,' he added with a wink.

I grinned slightly shamefacedly as I replied, 'You just go and get that cow in and have her ready for me. You couldn't have a nice lady like me walking through mucky fields. I'll be out to you as soon as we've finished swapping brown bread recipes.'

Washing out the cow with a mixture of antibiotics took much less time than it did to eat the dinner, and I found it equally difficult to do justice to the post-job feed. I thanked Mrs Roche as I was leaving and she took me warmly by both hands, 'Sure, don't you know you're always as welcome as any of the family, Gillian.'

As she withdrew her hands from mine, she brushed gently off a narrow band of metal on the third finger of my left hand. I noticed the sharp intake of breath and wondered if she was having an attack of angina.

I was surprised not to hear from the Roches for a while but I put it down to the peaceful spell that hits every yard now and again and the mild spell of weather we were having in the late autumn. It must have been six weeks before I heard Joe's voice on the other end of the phone.

'Dolly, the old Shorthorn, is a bit wobbly on her pins

after calving. Maybe you'd get a chance to drop up and have a look at her, Gillian.'

Excellent! I thought. A nice easy milk fever. I'd had an interrupted night, followed by a hectic day and the prospect of a good feed was tempting.

I was surprised when Mrs Roche didn't meet me at the door as usual. I made my way straight to the shed where I found Joe waiting. There lay Dolly, head twisted to one side, eyes dilated. I hardly needed to listen to the booming heart to confirm my diagnosis. A classic case of milk fever. As I watched the bottle of calcium bubble into Dolly's vein, Joe and I chatted away as usual. She was up before I had washed out the flutter valve. A contented belch assured me that all would be well.

'Come on in for some tea,' called Mrs Roche as she heard me washing my boots under the outdoor tap.

Although I enjoyed the freshly buttered tea brack, I noticed that the spread wasn't quite up to the normal standard and, although Mrs Roche was as talkative as usual, I thought she was less enthusiastic than on other occasions. I hoped she wasn't ill.

It was only after I had said my goodbyes and got back into the car that I noticed Slug was alone on the bare front seat. No half-dozen eggs, no scones, no tea-brack lest I grow weak on the fifteen-minute journey home. It was only then that I realised the damage that my wedding ring had done.

CHAPTER TWENTY-FIVE

A BUSY DAY

Gratefully, I collapsed into the ancient couch by the open fire in O'Neill's kitchen and then settled back to allow the blissful warmth to seep into my chilled bones. It was a bitterly cold December day and, perhaps in part due to a chronic lack of sleep, my body was refusing to adapt to the winter weather. As we were approaching Christmas, Donal was busy preparing the home-cured hams for which his family is famed. He worked from early morning and I worked late into the evening, so it seemed that we only ever met each other in passing.

It had been a long day, starting with a herd test of a hundred and eighty cattle, the majority of which were cows and so needed blood tests along with the routine TB test. By lunchtime, my arms ached from the effort of lifting up close to a hundred and fifty mucky tails as they lashed indignantly around my face. More than once, my frozen fingers lost their grip on the blood bottle and I watched in dismay as it disappeared into what was by then a well-filled dung channel, from which there was little hope of retrieving it. The book in which I painstakingly recorded the tag-number, sex, breed, skin measurements and blood bottle number of each animal became less and less legible as the morning progressed and, by the twelfth page, my pen had frozen solid and I had to resort to the pencil stub kept for such emergencies.

It didn't help that Martin, the farmer I was dealing with, was not one of the friendliest examples of a Wicklow farmer I had ever come across. I soon gave up on the light-hearted chat that usually helped pass such a morning. Worse still, when we finished, instead of the usual: 'You'll have a bite to eat,' the only comment was, 'I suppose you'll be a bit quicker reading them on Monday.' He then shoved a sheaf of tattered cards into my hand, which by that stage was so numb it felt as though it belonged to another body. I silently watched him as he tramped off to the house, and resolved to be late, in fact very late, on Monday morning.

Unused to having to fend for myself in such situations, I reluctantly made my way to the local café and wearily demolished a plate of beef stew. Before I had even managed to finish the cup of tea which followed, my mobile rang.

'Fergal Kennedy here. I've a cow calving this last few hours and I don't think she's making any progress. I reckon you might have to section her.'

'Well, you're usually right about that,' I answered, recalling the last two calls I had had from him. 'I'll be out to you within the half-hour.' Reluctantly, I pushed away the teapot.

Fergal was one of the new breed of young, progressive farmers who combined an agricultural background with an academic qualification and I knew from previous experience that he knew his stuff – I'd never yet had an easy calving in his yard.

It took an hour and a half of sustained effort before I was finally placing the last few sutures in his remarkably placid little Charolais heifer. She roughly licked the wet, leggy bull-calf as he struggled to stand beside her. At least the job had gone smoothly, with Fergal and his brother Eamon as able assistants. Better still, Eamon had gone to boil the kettle for a cup of tea while we finished up.

But it was not to be my day. Just as I was pulling off my gloves, the mobile rang. I had to concentrate to decipher the frantic flow of panic-sticken words from the other end.

'He's down and I don't know how long and he did this before and can you get the vet to come out quickly?'

With a bit of patience and calm talking, I managed to extract the vital details. The call was from the head groom in a horse-yard which I had often driven by, but never yet attended. One of the riding school ponies was 'rolling around in agony' and was definitely 'not going to last much longer!'

'Don't worry, I know where you are. I'll be with you in fifteen minutes.'

For the first time in the conversation there was a silence. 'Oh, are you a vet?' began the voice at the other end.

'Yes, I am. I've been with the practice for the last six months,' I replied.

'Well, are you any good with horses?' the voice asked suspiciously; the previous sense of urgency seeming to have suddenly abated.

'Well, I don't usually kill too many of them,' I replied smilingly, ignoring the bemused look on Fergal's face.

Another silence. A sense of humour was obviously not this person's strong point.

'I think maybe I might hold off until one of the real vets gets in.'

'That's fine. They're both off now for the weekend,' I replied blithely. 'You should catch them on Monday morning.' I pressed the end button, grinning at Fergal who by now had picked up the gist of the conversation.

'Right,' I said as I started scrubbing my instruments in the steaming hot water Eamon had left for me, 'I reckon about two minutes before they ring back.' It took only thirty seconds. I slowly and meticulously dried my hands, before finally picking up the phone. A quarter of an hour later, I was pulling into the stables.

Thankfully, the pony didn't seem to be too bad as I listened to the spasmodic rumbling in his gut. A quick history revealed that this particular pony was prone to colic and the three or four previous bouts had always occurred on a Friday evening. I knew the local girls' boarding school held a weekly 'camp' on Friday mornings so it was possibly a case of too many treats for this particularly handsome Palomino with his long, blond mane.

'Well, Starlight,' I said to him as I rooted through his rapidly thickening winter coat for a vein; I was confident that a mild anti-spasmodic was all that was required. 'For all your bimbo looks, you're smarter than I thought. I'm sure this will get you out of Saturday's riding lessons at least.' His gentle neighing gave nothing away.

I seemed to spend the rest of the day catching up. I was called out to attend another horse yard where a show-jumper had jumped out over a wire fence and suffered a gash the entire length of his cannon bone. The wound needed immediate stitching to have him right for a jumping qualifier less than three weeks away. It was a neat, fresh, wound that should have taken less than half an hour to treat, but Fireball was an excitable type. Despite the usual sedative and local anaesthetic and the soft whisperings of his owner, he fidgeted restlessly throughout, demanding a lot more patience than I felt I had left. By the time I was finished, it was after seven o' clock and when I got back to the surgery there was a fair-sized queue waiting outside for the evening clinic.

Luckily, most of my patients required nothing more demanding than a routine booster, with the exception of one miserable little Boxer pup who had been unfortunate enough to attend a birthday party for a five-year-old. He had spent the afternoon devouring rice-crispie cakes, jellies and birthday cake and was now suffering as a result.

By 8.30pm I was finally ready to wash the floors, turn off the lights and head home. I briefly contemplated stopping off for a takeaway but by now the day was beginning to take its toll on me. Despite Slug's hopeful face as we approached the local chipper, I just couldn't face getting out of the car and back into the icy wind. My mind switched off as I travelled the long road home. Then, just as I was almost there, the phone rang.

'Are you still at the surgery?' the caller inquired. I recognised the hearty tones of Barry O'Neill, a sheep farmer client of the practice.

'No, I'm actually at home now,' I answered cautiously. Please God, I thought to myself, let it be something that can wait until tomorrow. But no such luck.

'Oh, I am sorry,' he replied sincerely. 'I was hoping we would catch you before you left.'

'No problem. Don't worry about it,' I said, trying unsuccessfully to match his breezy tone. 'What can I do for you?'

'Well, the sheep were all fine when I checked them before tea but I've just been up to the shed and one of my Cheviot ewes is in trouble. Her bag is out a while but she isn't getting on with the job so I had a quick feel and all I can feel is a massive big head and no legs. I've lambed a few in my day,' he added, 'but this is definitely one for you lads.'

Without having ever hit home, I reversed the car into one of the neighbour's driveways and headed back down the hill. Barry had offered to bring the ewe into the surgery and, although I usually preferred that option, this time I decided against it, as his yard was nearer. By now, Donal had long since given up believing me when I would ring to say I was on my way home. He wasn't long in himself and he didn't sound surprised when I rang to tell him I would be at least another hour.

I have often been pleasantly surprised at being able to deliver what appeared to be a hopeless case, but I knew the minute I felt the head that this lamb was going nowhere. He was well and truly stuck. Barry opted for a caesarean and, while I was glad of the chance to do it, as up to now I had only done one on a sheep, I just wished that it could have been tomorrow morning instead.

Once I had the ewe set up on a few bales of straw that were to serve as my operating table, with Barry and his son Peter restraining her, I warmed to the job. I was relieved to remember how much easier it was to section a ewe than a cow. Before long, the sheep lay resting on her side, displaying a neat row of sutures, with two thriving lambs by her side.

'Well, that's a job well done anyway,' said Barry's wife Eithne, who had joined us to check on progress.

'It surely is,' said Barry, 'and would you believe that Gillian hasn't even finished her lunch yet, never mind her dinner? We'd better rustle up something to keep the bill down!'

While I injected some antibiotic into the ewe, Barry started to rinse my instruments in a fresh bucket of hot water. By now, I was so exhausted that I didn't try to stop him. Half an hour crouched over a sheep in a shed had allowed the cold to penetrate deep into my body and I was suddenly ravenous.

Once I had washed and removed my overalls, I sank thankfully into a comfortable armchair, to gaze trance-like into the dancing flames of the open fire as its radiant warmth gradually penetrated me. I wondered how I would find the energy to drive home again.

By the time I had polished off the 'quick snack' that Eithne had miraculously put together, I was feeling decidedly mellow and the quiet contentment of a successful day was beginning to make me feel at one with the world again. Just as I was beginning to luxuriate in this comfortable state of affairs, my phone rang again. I laughed resignedly as my hosts commiserated.

Reluctantly, I dragged myself out of the chair and headed back to the cold jeep. Oh well, at least it's only a cow with an uncomplicated milk fever. In and out in fifteen minutes, I told myself.

Fitzpatricks in Annacurragh. I hadn't been to them before, but Barry had given me directions. I should find it easily enough and it was only ten minutes away, heading in the right direction for home.

The crisp cold of the winter's night quickly woke me up and, with a full stomach, my spirits were rejuvenated. As I drove along the rapidly freezing roads, I replayed the events of the day in my mind. Despite all the ups and downs of my first year, I was beginning to feel like a real vet. Look at today, I reminded myself. A difficult herd test, a cow caesarean, a colic, a horse stitch-up, a sheep caesarean, difficult clients – not a bother to you! I congratulated myself. Finally, I felt I was beginning to make my mark on the veterinary world – a fully-fledged veterinary surgeon had emerged!

By the time I reached Annacurragh, I was brimming with confidence and the warm glow of contentment in which I was basking seemed to dispel even the icy chill of the winter's night. Up ahead, I saw a yard entrance with a five-bar gate and then a shed up on the hill as described by Tom Fitzpatrick over the phone.

I strode confidently up to the shed. Not for me, anymore, the apprehension of meeting new clients; sure, why wouldn't they be impressed by so exemplary a representative of the veterinary profession as myself?

A few hollers around the yard produced no results and I

was slightly surprised to have to knock on the kitchen door.

I had to knock a second time before an elderly man appeared and pulled open the heavy door.

'Gillian, the vet,' I informed him as I grasped his hand and forcefully pumped it up and down. I waited. 'Right so,' I said, 'I'll head on up to the shed, if you want to follow when you're ready.'

Not a very talkative type, I thought to myself, as I pulled open the double doors of the two-span shed and felt around for the light switch. I drew out the bottle of calcium and attached it to the flutter-valve. Most of the cattle were looking around, blinking painfully against the harsh glare of the fluorescent lights. Although there were only twenty or so cows, I couldn't readily pick out my patient. I stamped around impatiently until the old man poked his head around the door.

'Can I help you at all?' he asked, looking at me a bit strangely.

'No, I'm all set up here. If you could just point out the cow, I'll be out of your way in no time.'

'The cow?' he repeated stupidly, a blank expression on his wizened face.

'Yes, yes, the one with the milk fever,' I explained impatiently, as I squeezed the rubber base of the flutter valve to start the sticky liquid flowing.

'A cow with milk fever? We don't have a cow with milk fever,' he replied, beginning to look slightly worried as he eyed my loaded pockets suspiciously.

'Tom Fitzpatrick. Annacurragh. You were on to me not

twenty minutes ago. You have a cow with milk fever,' I repeated slowly and patiently, beginning to wonder if the elderly man was suffering from amnesia.

There was a pause as he stared at me, then gradually the worried look was replaced by a slow twitch of his mouth and a twinkling in his eye and I got the impression that he was about to laugh. 'Tom Fitzpatrick. Annacurragh,' he repeated as he slowly took me by the arm and led me out to the door of the shed before pointing towards a large dairy, barely discernible by its glowing lights, further down the valley. 'That's his yard down there.'

It took a few seconds for what he was saying to sink in; much less for the deep red flush to start rising from my neck and over my face.

'Oh, I'm so sorry,' I muttered, my newfound confidence bursting like a bubble as I began to shove the flutter valve back into the side pocket of my overalls.

'You see, I don't really know the area and I thought you were him, and ...' I trailed off lamely as I noticed that the man was chuckling away.

'Always the same, you vets are!' he laughed. 'Always rushing!'

This time I didn't need to switch on the heat as I sped back down the driveway.

Within half an hour, I had completed the job, this time in the correct yard, and if the real Tom Fitzpatrick found me slightly uncommunicative it was because I spent my time imagining him talking with his elderly neighbour and the laughter that would ensue between the two of them the following morning.

EPILOGUE

It seemed like only the other day that I had done my very first bitch spay and now here I was again: the sickly feeling of apprehension and the sweaty palms as the premedication was injected into the little terrier, handpicked for the job – small and light, not carrying any excessive amounts of fat. Should be a nice one, but still …

My instruments were carefully laid out, by now showing some signs of wear and tear, but lovingly maintained – my shining comrades throughout the previous year.

The little dog was now fast asleep. 'It'll be over soon now,' I whispered reassuringly to my patient, as if to reassure myself too.

The sharp scalpel blade sliced cleanly through the prepared site. 'Good start.' I nodded approvingly, although feeling perhaps it could have gone a bit deeper.

As expected, not much fat but still the thin white band that was the intended site through which to open into the abdomen seemed stubbornly elusive. Time seemed to stand still before a tiny nick in the body wall became apparent and the glistening organs peeped through.

'Now, just the tip of the scissors,' I reminded, suddenly wondering why I was whispering. I watched carefully to ensure that the sharp points stayed well clear of the delicate organs beneath the muscle layer.

The relaxed, even breathing of the little dog calmed me as I watched, conscious of the air of enthusiasm and yet oh so aware of its tender fragility.

Soon, the first ovary had been clamped, tied off and cut with only the faintest hint of a shaking hand. I held my breath as the clamp was released, half expecting the spurt of blood from a loosened vessel – but there was none. Relief. But only for as long as it took to start on the other side. Over to the right now, always more difficult – delicately pulling at the ligament, not knowing just at what moment it would snap.

I could feel a niggling ache in my back from sheer tension as the jaws of the forceps stubbornly refused to go around the pedicle of the deeper ovary. Repeated attempts to slide the instrument down along the vessel were unsuccessful, always managing to ensnare an extra piece of tissue that just shouldn't be there. The loops of gut stubbornly refused to stay out of the way, despite careful pushing with a sterile swab.

'This is always the hardest bit,' I proclaimed with an air of forced gaiety. 'Once this bit's done, the rest is easy.'

But no, this time the clamp was too high up, leaving a section of the tiny ovary within its jaws. By now, a feeling of desperation was in danger of creeping in. I forced myself to be calm.

Patience, I urged myself, taking a deep breath and trying to stay light-hearted.

This time, easing the forceps way down into the abdomen, closely following the vessels that were clearly visible through the fat and – there, that had to be it! Jaws securely clamped. The second forceps, always easier now. Now, cut the ovary and then a good inspection from all angles to ensure that all is well.

With clammy fingers, delicately holding the remaining stump, the clamp released and there it was, no bleeding as it slithered back down into the depths of the abdomen. By the time the uterus was tied off, the tension was beginning to clear. With only the stitch-up to go, the hard work was over and the buzz of anticipation began to build up again. The pleasure of a job well done, heightened by the anxiety felt before. The layers of muscle came together nicely with the neat simple sutures and I carefully snipped off the ends to the required length. Not much fat to realign but, for practice, a subcutaneous layer. Not so great, I thought, as a little knobble of skin that didn't quite match up was formed at one end. No, let it go, I advised myself.

'Excellent job,' I declared out loud, pulling off the blood-stained drapes. 'After that one going so nicely, you'll find the rest of them easy,' I said to my student, Orla. She smiled, looking relieved. She had completed her first bitch spay with, by the looks of her, less nerves than I, who had merely supervised.

It was hard to believe that in such a short space of time I had gone from supervisee to supervisor and I felt a sense of pride that a student of my own was now setting out on the same path that I had taken. Who knew what the future held in store for either of us?